DRAMA CLASSICS

The Drama Classics series aims to offer the world's greatest plays in affordable paperback editions for students, actors and theatregoers. The hallmarks of the series are accessible introductions, uncluttered texts and an overall theatrical perspective.

Given that readers may be encountering a particular play for the first time, the introduction seeks to fill in the theatrical/historical background and to outline the chief themes rather than concentrate on interpretational and textual analysis. Similarly the play-texts themselves are free of footnotes and other interpolations: instead there is an end-glossary of 'difficult' words and phrases.

The texts of the English-language plays in the series have been prepared taking full account of all existing scholarship. The foreign-language plays have been newly translated into a modern English that is both actable and accurate: many of the translators regularly have their work staged professionally.

Edited until his early death by Kenneth McLeish, the Drama Classics series continues with his aim of providing a first-class library of dramatic literature representing the best of world theatre.

Associate editors:
Professor Trevor R. Griffiths
Dr. Colin Counsell
School of Arts and Humanities
University of North London

DRAMA CLASSICS *the first hundred*

The Alchemist
All for Love
Andromache
Antigone
Arden of Faversham
Bacchae
Bartholomew Fair
The Beaux Stratagem
The Beggar's Opera
Birds
The Changeling
A Chaste Maid in
  Cheapside
The Cherry Orchard
Children of the Sun
El Cid
The Country Wife
Cyrano de Bergerac
The Dance of Death
The Devil is an
  Ass
Doctor Faustus
A Doll's House
Don Juan
The Duchess of
  Malfi
Edward II
Electra (Euripides)
Electra (Sophocles)
An Enemy of the
  People
Every Man in his
  Humour
Everyman
The Father
Faust
A Flea in her Ear
Frogs
Fuenteovejuna
The Game of Love
  and Chance
Ghosts

The Government
  Inspector
Hedda Gabler
The Hypochondriac
The Importance of
  Being Earnest
An Ideal Husband
An Italian Straw Hat
The Jew of Malta
The Knight of the
  Burning Pestle
The Lady from the Sea
The Learned Ladies
Lady Windermere's
  Fan
Life is a Dream
The Lower Depths
The Lucky Chance
Lulu
Lysistrata
The Magistrate
The Malcontent
The Man of Mode
The Marriage of
  Figaro
Mary Stuart
The Master Builder
Medea
The Misanthrope
The Miser
Miss Julie
A Month in the
  Country
A New Way to Pay
  Old Debts
Oedipus
The Oresteia
Peer Gynt
Phedra
Philoctetes
The Playboy of the
  Western World

The Recruiting Officer
The Revenger's
  Tragedy
The Rivals
The Roaring Girl
La Ronde
Rosmersholm
The Rover
The School for
  Scandal
The Seagull
The Servant of Two
  Masters
She Stoops to
  Conquer
The Shoemaker's
  Holiday
Six Characters in Search
  of an Author
The Spanish Tragedy
Spring's Awakening
Summerfolk
Tartuffe
Thérèse Raquin
Three Sisters
'Tis Pity She's a
  Whore
Too Clever by Half
Ubu
Uncle Vanya
Volpone
The Way of the
  World
The White Devil
The Wild Duck
Women Beware
  Women
Women of Troy
Woyzeck

*The publishers welcome
suggestions for further titles*

DRAMA CLASSICS

ROSMERSHOLM

by

Henrik Ibsen

translated by Kenneth McLeish

with an introduction by Stephen Mulrine

NICK HERN BOOKS
London

www.nickhernbooks.co.uk

A Drama Classic

Rosmersholm first published in Great Britain in this translation
as a paperback original in 2003 by Nick Hern Books Limited,
14 Larden Road, London W3 7ST

Copyright in the Introduction © 2003 by Nick Hern Books Ltd

Copyright in this translation from Norwegian © 2003
by the Estate of the late Kenneth McLeish

Typeset by Country Setting, Kingsdown, Kent CT14 8ES
Printed by Bookmarque, Croydon, Surrey

A CIP catalogue record for this book is available from
the British Library

ISBN 1 85459 644 6

Introduction

Henrik Ibsen (1828-1906)

Henrik Ibsen was born on 20 March 1828 in Skien, a small town to the south of Kristiania (modern Oslo), into a prosperous middle-class family. His mother, Marichen, took a lively interest in the arts, and Ibsen was introduced to the theatre at an early age. When he was six, however, his father's business failed, and Ibsen's childhood was spent in relative poverty, until he was forced to leave school and find employment as an apprentice pharmacist in Grimstad. In 1846, an affair with a housemaid ten years his senior produced an illegitimate son, whose upbringing Ibsen was compelled to pay for until the boy was in his teens, though he saw nothing of him. Ibsen's family relationships in general were not happy, and after the age of twenty-two, he never saw either of his parents again, and kept in touch with them only through his sister Hedvig's letters.

While still working as a pharmacist, Ibsen was studying for university, in pursuit of a vague ambition to become a doctor. He failed the entrance examination, however, and at the age of twenty launched his literary career with the publication in 1850 of a verse play, *Catiline*, which sold a mere fifty copies, having already been rejected by the Danish Theatre in Kristiania. Drama in Norwegian, as opposed to Swedish and Danish, was virtually non-existent at this time, and the low status of the language reflected Norway's own position, as a province of Denmark, for most of the preceding five centuries. Kristiania, the capital, was one of Europe's smallest, with fewer than 30,000 inhabitants, and communications were primitive.

However, change, as far as the theatre was concerned, was already under way, and Ibsen and his younger contemporary Bjørnson were among the prime movers. Another was the internationally famous violinist, Ole Bull, who founded a Norwegian-language theatre in his home town of Bergen, and invited Ibsen to become its first resident dramatist in 1851, with a commitment to write one play each year, to be premièred on January 2nd, the anniversary of the theatre's founding.

During his time at Bergen, Ibsen wrote five plays, mainly historical in content: *St. John's Night*, a comedy which he later disowned, loosely based on *A Midsummer Night's Dream*; *The Warrior's Barrow*, a reworking of a one-act verse play first staged in Kristiania; *Lady Inger of Østråt*, a five-act drama set in 16th-century Trondheim, on the theme of Norwegian independence; *The Feast at Solhaug*, which went on to be commercially published; and a romantic drama, *Olaf Liljekrans*, to complete his contractual obligations in Bergen.

Ibsen had meanwhile met his future wife, Suzannah Thoresen, and the offer of a post as artistic director of the newly-created Norwegian Theatre in Kristiania must have been very welcome. Ibsen took up his post in September 1857, with a specific remit to compete for audiences with the long-established Danish Theatre in Kristiania. A successful first season was accordingly crucial, and his own new play, *The Vikings at Helgeland*, set in 10th-century Norway, and based on material drawn from the Norse sagas, was an important contribution. By 1861, however, the Danish Theatre was clearly winning the battle, in part by extending its Norwegian repertoire, and Ibsen's theatre was forced to close, in the summer of 1862.

Now unemployed, Ibsen successfully applied for a government grant to collect folk-tales in the Norwegian hinterland. During this period he also wrote *Love's Comedy*, a verse play on the theme of modern marriage, and a five-act historical drama, *The Pretenders*, now regarded as his first major play, premièred at the Kristiania Theatre in January 1864, under Ibsen's own direction. A few months later, financed by another government grant, Ibsen left Norway for Copenhagen on 2 April 1864, beginning a journey that would take him on to Rome, and international recognition.

Brand, the first fruit of Ibsen's self-imposed exile, sees him abandoning historical themes, and drawing on his own experience more directly, basing his uncompromising hero on a fanatical priest who had led a religious revival in Ibsen's home town of Skien in the 1850's. Like all of Ibsen's plays, *Brand* was published before it was staged, in March 1866, and received its first full performance almost twenty years later, in 1885 at the Nya Theatre in Stockholm, though it seems clear that like *Peer Gynt*, his next play, *Brand* was intended to be read, rather than acted.

Ibsen wrote *Peer Gynt* at Rome, Ischia and Sorrento, through the summer of 1867, using material from Asbjørnsen's recently-published *Norwegian Folk-Tales*, as well as the darker corners of his own life, but the end result is regarded as containing some of his finest dramatic writing, with the irrepressible Peer at the other end of the moral spectrum from Brand, a typical example of Ibsen's fondness for opposites or antitheses in his dramatic work.

The following spring, Ibsen left Rome for Berchtesgaden in the Bavarian Alps, to work on a new play, *The League of*

Youth, which was premièred at the Kristiania Theatre in October 1869, and attracted some hostility for its satirical portrayal of contemporary politicians. A few weeks later, Ibsen travelled to Egypt, to represent his country at the official opening of the Suez Canal.

On his return, Ibsen began work on what he regarded as his greatest achievement, the mammoth ten-act *Emperor and Galilean*, dramatising the conflict between Christianity and paganism, through the life of Julian the Apostate. Published in Copenhagen in October 1873, to critical acclaim, the play nonetheless had to wait over a century before it was staged in full, an eight-hour marathon in Oslo in 1987.

By this time, Ibsen's fame had brought him tempting offers to return to Norway, as well as recognition at the highest level in the form of a knighthood, of the Order of St Olaf. However, apart from a brief sojourn in Kristiania in the summer of 1874, he remained in Germany, moving from Dresden to Munich the following year, to commence writing *Pillars of the Community*, completed in 1877, the first in a series of 'social problem' plays, although its large cast requirements make it nowadays something of a theatrical rarity. By contrast, his next play, *A Doll's House*, has seldom been absent from the stage since its Copenhagen première in December 1879, and the challenge it offers to male hypocrisy and so-called 'family values' has ensured its continuing popularity.

In Ibsen's characteristic manner, *Ghosts* in effect is the obverse of *A Doll's House*. Whereas in the latter play Nora flees the family home, in *Ghosts* Ibsen shows the tragic consequences of a wife's failure to break free from a disastrous marriage. Its exposure of taboo subjects like venereal disease, however, still retains the power to shock, and it was at first rejected by all Ibsen's preferred theatres.

After publication in 1881, almost two years elapsed before *Ghosts* was staged in Scandinavia, the world première having already taken place in Chicago, in May 1882.

Ibsen was angered by his countrymen's reception of *Ghosts*, and *An Enemy of the People*, with its ill-concealed attack on the Norwegian establishment, is to an extent a vehicle for that anger, as well as for Ibsen's sceptical views on democracy. The play thus offended liberals and conservatives alike, but not enough to impede its staging, and it was premièred in Kristiania in January 1883, to mixed reviews.

The initial reaction to *The Wild Duck*, published in November of the following year, was largely one of bewilderment, although it was produced without delay in all the major Scandinavian venues. While the 'original sin' of the drama, the housemaid made pregnant by her master and married off to a convenient dupe, echoes that of *Ghosts*, Ibsen's use of symbolism appeared to sit uneasily with the naturalistic dialogue, and indeed still troubles modern audiences.

However, Ibsen was moving away from the concerns of the 'problem play' towards a more personal, oblique utterance, and the controversy which dogged his work scarcely lessened with the publication of *Rosmersholm*, in November 1886, following a brief return to Norway, after an eleven-year absence. Partly inspired by Ibsen's disillusionment with Norwegian politics, it is especially noteworthy for the creation of Rebecca West, one of his most compelling characters, though its witches' brew of ingredients caused something of a scandal.

Ibsen's reputation was by now unassailable, however, and in Germany particularly, the innovative productions of the Saxe-Meiningen company had won him an eager following.

In England, the enthusiasm of Edmund Gosse, and later William Archer, ensured that several of his plays were at least available in print in translation, but the first significant staging of his work in London had to wait until June 1889, with the Novelty Theatre production of *A Doll's House*.

Meanwhile, *The Lady from the Sea* fared well enough at the box office, with simultaneous premières in Kristiania and Weimar, on 12 February, 1889, though again its complex amalgam of dreamy symbolism, evolutionary theory, and the daily routine of the Wangel household in northern Norway, tended to confuse audiences, and is still something of an obstacle to production.

Hedda Gabler, premièred in Munich at the Residenztheater in January 1891, is now Ibsen's most popular play, but attracted fierce criticism in its day, largely on account of the character of Hedda herself. Arguably Ibsen's finest creation, Hedda's contempt for the sacred roles of wife and mother seemed the more offensive in that Ibsen provided no explanation for it, no inherited moral taint, and she continues to unnerve us even today, like a glimpse into the abyss.

In that same year, 1891, there were no fewer than five London productions of Ibsen plays, including *Hedda Gabler*, and the publication of George Bernard Shaw's seminal critique, *The Quintessence of Ibsenism*, helped assure his place in the permanent English repertoire. Ibsen himself finally returned to Norway in July, a national hero, though he suffered the indignity of hearing his achievement disparaged by the rising young novelist Knut Hamsun, at a public lecture in October.

In his declining years, Ibsen increasingly sought the company of young female admirers, and his relationships with Emilie Bardach, Helene Raff, and finally Hildur

Andersen, find their way into his later plays, notably *The Master Builder*, in which Ibsen also revisits the theme of self, which had inspired his early masterpieces, *Brand* and *Peer Gynt*. The burden of fame, the generational conflict between age and youth, Ibsen's personal concerns, are all explored in the relationship between the successful middle-aged architect Solness and the twenty-something 'free spirit' Hilde Wangel. Although the all-pervasive tower metaphor puzzled some critics, given that Freud had still to explain such things, the play was an instant success, going on from its première in Berlin in January 1893, to productions in Scandinavia, Paris, Chicago and London within the year.

Ibsen's next play, *Little Eyolf*, despite having the distinction of a public reading in English, at the Haymarket Theatre in December 1893, even before it was published in Copenhagen, has enjoyed little success on the stage, where its mixed modes of realism and symbolism can fail to blend, with unintentionally comic results. However, *John Gabriel Borkman*, published three years later, and premièred in Helsinki in January 1897, achieves in prose the poetic grandeur of *Brand*. The play is drawn in part from Ibsen's own experience of humiliating dependency, in the wake of his father's financial ruin, and explores Ibsen's cherished themes, the corrupting influence of materialism, personal freedom and self-doubt, and marital disharmony.

Ibsen was now permanently resident in Kristiania, venerated wherever he went, and his seventieth birthday, on 20 March 1898, was the occasion for widespread rejoicing. His collected works were in preparation in both Denmark and Germany, and his international fame rivalled that of Tolstoy. It is fitting, therefore, that Ibsen's last play, *When We Dead Awaken*, should have been premièred on 15 January 1900, in effect launching the next century, at Kristiania's new National Theatre, the confident expression of that Norwegian identity which Ibsen and Bjørnson, whose statues graced its entrance, did so much to promote.

Finally, like almost all of Ibsen's plays, *When We Dead Awaken* is a response to the author's psychic needs, part confession, part exorcism, and it can be argued that the ageing sculptor Rubek's return to his first inspiration, Irene, now confined in a sanatorium, represents Ibsen's feelings of guilt over his neglect of his wife Suzannah, and his belated acknowledgement that she had been the real sustaining force behind his work. The tone of *When We Dead Awaken* is accordingly elegiac, an appropriate coda to Ibsen's long career. Two months later, in March 1900, he suffered the first of a series of strokes which was to lead to his death, in Kristiania, on 23 May 1906.

Rosmersholm: **What Happens in the Play**

The action of the play takes place at Rosmersholm, the Rosmer family estate; Act One is set in the drawing-room, hung with ancestral portraits. Rebecca West, formerly companion to Johannes Rosmer's late wife Beata, in conversation with the housekeeper Mrs Helseth, learns of a local superstition – a mysterious white horse, said to appear when a Rosmer is about to die, and they reflect on the powerful influence exerted by the dead on the living at Rosmersholm, until an unexpected visitor, Doctor Kroll, arrives. Kroll is the local headmaster, Rosmer's brother-in-law, and he remarks first on the flower-bedecked room (his late sister couldn't bear them), before gently trying to persuade Rebecca that her place is now with the widowed Rosmer, in Beata's stead. However, Kroll and Rebecca are poles apart politically, and his reactionary conservatism is certain to cause friction, set against Rebecca's own enlightened views, especially when Rosmer arrives, and Kroll reveals that his purpose in coming to Rosmersholm is to win his brother-in-law to the conservative cause, offering him the editorship of a right-wing newspaper.

What Kroll does not know is that Rebecca has already changed Rosmer's way of thinking, but the latter is reluctant to dispute with Kroll, and excuses himself on the grounds of inadequacy, somewhat to Rebecca's displeasure. They are then interrupted by the arrival of Ulrik Brendel, a controversial writer and activist, who had once been Rosmer's tutor, until driven from the house by Rosmer's domineering father, for his radical opinions. Brendel is paying an unexpected visit to his old haunts, and plans to give a series of lectures in town on the theme of democracy. Rebecca is impressed, Kroll predictably contemptuous. After borrowing some money and clothes, Brendel leaves. Alone now with Kroll, Rosmer finally admits the reason for his reluctance to assist his brother-in-law – his political outlook has changed, and he is now committed to the progressive cause. Kroll is dismayed, and promptly declares that his friendship with Rosmer is over. As Kroll leaves, he is on the point of making some wounding remark about Rebecca, but thinks better of it.

At the beginning of Act Two, the following morning, Rebecca confesses to Rosmer that she has given Brendel an introduction to one Peder Mortensgård, the editor of a local radical newspaper. Rosmer questions the wisdom of her action, but before they can discuss its implications, an angry Kroll arrives with news of Brendel's scandalous conduct in town the previous night, extending to a drunken brawl. Kroll demands to speak with Rosmer alone, and reveals to him that Rebecca was to blame for his wife's suicide – that believing Rebecca was pregnant by Rosmer, Beata drowned herself in order to free him to marry Rebecca, and save his reputation. Beata's anguish, furthermore, was the more intense because of Rosmer's inability to respond to her passion, and her own failure to bear him a child.

Kroll goes on to question the morality of Rosmer and the free-thinking Rebecca living under the same roof, since she is evidently a corrupting influence on him. Rosmer, however, announces his intention to pursue his new-found ideals, whatever the cost. At this point, they are interrupted by the arrival of Mortensgård, Kroll's sworn enemy, and after an exchange of insults, Kroll storms out. Mortensgård tells Rosmer that he has come to thank Rebecca for assisting Brendel, and is both surprised and delighted to learn of Rosmer's new political allegiance. Rosmer and he have a past history of enmity, but the declared support of a respected practising Christian will be a great propaganda coup for his party. In consequence, Mortensgård receives the news that Rosmer has also broken with the Church rather less enthusiastically. He agrees to publicise Rosmer's political conversion, but not his break with the Church, and after warning Rosmer that he must expect to be pilloried in the reactionary press, reveals that he himself possesses a letter, sent by Rosmer's late wife Beata, which seems to lend substance to rumours of an affair between Rosmer and Rebecca.

After Mortensgård departs, Rebecca appears from behind the curtains, where she has overheard everything, including Kroll's accusation. Rosmer agonises over his treatment of Beata, even though there was no affair, and seems on the point of abandoning his new convictions. Finally, he decides that the only way to be meaningfully alive, and exorcise Beata's ghost, is to marry Rebecca. To his consternation,

Rebecca rejects his proposal, and refuses to give a reason. Indeed, if Rosmer should ever ask her again, she declares, she will follow Beata's tragic example and kill herself.

Act Three opens with a conversation between Rebecca and Mrs Helseth, in which the housekeeper recalls having delivered the compromising letter from Beata to Mortensgård, and declares her own belief that it was Kroll's wife who had been responsible for poisoning Beata's mind about the relationship between Rosmer and Rebecca. Rosmer then enters, and Rebecca shows him that day's copy of the local right-wing newspaper, which contains a scurrilous attack on him. Unknown to Rosmer, meanwhile, Kroll has arrived at the house, to seek a private meeting with Rebecca.

Alone with Rebecca, Kroll immediately goes on the offensive, laying the blame for Rosmer's political conversion, and his loss of faith, squarely at Rebecca's door. Somewhat to his discomfiture, she reminds him that his opinion of her was once very different, but he accuses her of having bewitched everyone she came in contact with, including the unfortunate Beata. Kroll then contrasts Rosmer's distinguished family history with Rebecca's own, suggesting that her immoral character is an inherited trait, and that she herself was the product of an adulterous liaison between her mother, and a certain Dr West, who became Rebecca's guardian after her mother's death. This Rebecca vehemently denies, but her show of emotion only serves to confirm his belief. Kroll's principal concern, however, is for Rosmer's reputation, not hers, and he urges her to marry Rosmer, to legalise their relationship. Rebecca then sends for Rosmer and insists that Kroll stay to hear what she has to say.

When Rosmer enters, she tells him that she intends to restore him to his state of innocence, to relieve him of the burden of guilt he bears over his wife's suicide. Rebecca now confesses that she had purposely sought to release him from the spiritual prison of his marriage to Beata. Rosmer is blameless, it was she alone who set Beata on the fatal path that led to the mill-race in which she drowned herself. Rebecca also claims to have persuaded Beata that it was her duty to set Rosmer free. Rosmer is horrified by this revelation, and promptly leaves with Kroll, his new-found political idealism effectively dead, before it could be tested. Rebecca then informs Mrs Helseth that she is quitting the house for good. Ominously, Rebecca has had a vision of the mysterious white horses of Rosmersholm, said to appear when a death is imminent.

At the beginning of Act Four, Rebecca is making ready to leave Rosmersholm by the night steamer. Mrs Helseth is angry, believing that Rosmer has walked out on Rebecca because she is pregnant. Rosmer returns home, however, having made his peace with Kroll and his former friends, convinced now that he is simply not up to the great work Rebecca had mapped out for him, of reforming society. Rebecca tries to explain further her actions, describing how her plans for Rosmer had been overtaken by her growing passion for him, which had led her to destroy Beata. And when Rosmer had asked her to marry him, she had refused because the morbid atmosphere of Rosmersholm had killed her spirit. Rosmer again offers to marry her, and again she rejects him, hinting at something in her past much worse than illegitimacy. Their conversation then turns to the topic of a genuinely unselfish love, and its power to ennoble people. Rosmer cannot believe that Rebecca's love for him is of this kind, and he asks her for proof. At this point, Ulrik Brendel enters, on his way downhill, as he says, towards oblivion – resigned now to a life without ideals, in which only such as Peder Mortensgård can survive.

After Brendel's departure, Rosmer gives serious thought to the idea of suicide, as a solution to his moral inertia. Rebecca urges him to continue the fight, but Rosmer cannot believe he has the power to change anyone's life – that is, unless Rebecca were to follow Beata's tragic example, and sacrifice herself, as proof of her love for him, something which Brendel had half-jokingly suggested. Rebecca calmly agrees, and a strangely excited Rosmer makes up his mind to accompany her. Hand in hand, they walk out of the house towards the mill-race, playing out a symbolic marriage, before hurling themselves into the rushing water, and Beata's deathly embrace.

Rosmersholm: the Political and the Personal

Rosmersholm is a transitional work, bringing to a close the series of socially committed plays, begun in 1877 with *Pillars of the Community*, and inaugurating a new phase in Ibsen's dramatic career, fully expressed by *The Lady From the Sea*, which followed *Rosmersholm* in 1888, and unwaveringly maintained until his final work, *When We Dead Awaken*, in 1899. In Ibsen's later plays the focus shifts from the representative type, actively engaged in political and social relationships, to the unique individual, acted upon by private fears and desires, with an inner life of indescribable complexity, revealed only in glimpses.

That shift of focus, from the political to the personal, occurs during the course of *Rosmersholm* itself, and the play in a sense records Ibsen's disenchantment with the Norwegian political scene, as he observed it in the summer of 1885, on a brief visit to his homeland following an eleven-year absence. On the surface, Norway was a democracy: a longstanding conflict between the royally-appointed cabinet and the elected parliament, the Storthing, in which the liberals were in the majority, had been resolved in the liberals' favour the year before Ibsen's return. However, the two parties were very far from reconciled, to the extent that Ibsen could acidly describe the country as being populated by two million cats and dogs. Political strife divided families, reflected in the play by the rift between the reactionary Kroll and his children, and while Ibsen's own allegiances lay well left of centre, his impatience with party politics in general can be seen in his treatment of Kroll's polar opposite, the left-wing journalist Peder Mortensgård, all too ready to compromise his principles, to win the 'Christian' vote.

Increasingly, Ibsen had come to distrust political institutions, from which ordinary working men and women, in particular, were effectively excluded. The genuine commitment of so-called anarchists and nihilists was another matter, but Ibsen was also sceptical of the utopian dreamer, represented here by Ulrik Brendel, temperamentally incapable of translating his inspiring words into action. Addressing a workers' meeting at Trondheim on 14 June 1885, Ibsen virtually mapped out the political scenario of *Rosmersholm*, attacking the sham democracy of Norway's party system, and calling for a new kind of aristocracy, not of privileged birth or wealth, but of true nobility of spirit. Ibsen is under no illusions about the magnitude of the task, which demands nothing less than the moral regeneration of each individual, but that is the goal Johannes Rosmer sets for himself, awakened into active life by Rebecca West, out of the deep ancestral sleep of Rosmersholm.

Rosmer speaks for Ibsen in all this, but the political debate in *Rosmersholm*, though it supplies a gritty realistic texture to the play, is secondary to the main drama, which is profoundly psychological – a study of the hidden springs of action, and especially the impact of the past, remembered or forgotten, on the present. Rosmer's past is plain to see, made physical in the family portraits crowding the walls of the play's single, claustrophobic room setting. It is moreover no accident that much of the first act is taken up with the 'old' Rosmer, defined for us by Kroll and Ulrik Brendel, in their different ways, while the 'new' Rosmer of the present, re-made by Rebecca, is unveiled only towards the end.

As Kroll storms out, breaking off his friendship with Rosmer, his last words appear to call Rebecca's past in question; Ibsen's characteristic 'onionskin' method is patently under way. Early reference is made to the presence of the dead at Rosmersholm, and while the tragic suicide of his wife Beata continues to trouble Rosmer's conscience, Kroll's unfinished jibe suggests that Rebecca is also culpable. By contrast with Rosmer, the last of his distinguished line, however, Rebecca's past is largely concealed. Like the mysterious Stranger in *The Lady From the Sea*, she comes from Finmark, in the remote north, out of nowhere in effect, and apart from hints of a dubious relationship with her guardian Dr West, we know very little about her. In a Norwegian context, Finmark is a rich source of folklore, and the fact that in Act III, Rebecca specifies a sealskin trunk for her packing, suggests an identification with the seal-woman of legend, who must retrieve her skin, before she can leave her human husband and return to her proper element. As the play moves from politics to individuals, however, what lies beneath the sealskin is slowly brought to light, beginning with Rebecca's admission of her all too-human purpose in conspiring to drive Beata to her death.

Rosmersholm: **Dramatic Technique**

Rosmersholm has been described as the most perfect
expression of Ibsen's mature technique, in which the past
constantly erupts into the present, not as narrative, but as
potent drama, changing relationships and influencing action
at every turn. It is so at the pivotal moment in Act II,
when Rosmer's offer of marriage to Rebecca is at first
joyfully accepted, then almost in the same breath refused.
Rosmer's proposal has less to do with sexual passion,
however, than his desire to slough off his past, to remove
the corpse from his back, as he puts it, in order to enter the
stream of life. Rebecca cannot escape her past either, but
her guilt in the matter of Beata's suicide is only the first,
conscious layer. As the play develops, Ibsen's lance probes
her psychic wound ever deeper, until the long buried taint
of incest is reached, and we know there can be no future
for the pair. In a sense, the real drama of *Rosmersholm* takes
place in the characters' subconscious, at a time when the
term had only limited currency, some thirty years before
Sigmund Freud's classic study of the fictional Rebecca, as
an example of the Oedipus complex. Broadly, the guiding
principle of psychoanalysis is that the past must be
remembered, in order to be forgotten, and that is made
abundantly clear in *Rosmersholm*.

In the dramatic canon of star-crossed lovers, Rosmer and
Rebecca are surely extraordinary. Not until the final scene,
when they link hands to walk out to their deaths, do they
even touch one another, and yet the intensity of their
relationship is such that they almost exchange souls. Driven
on by Rebecca, Rosmer attempts to break out of his
ancestral cocoon – that Rosmersholm in which children
never cry, nor adults laugh – into the living world.
Unhappily, his metamorphosis is spoiled by an

acknowledgement of guilt, calling in question his credentials as a power for good in the world; Rebecca, on the other hand, the irresistible force, has absorbed so much of Rosmersholm, its ancient moral code, and Rosmer's own nobility of spirit, into her bloodstream, as to impair her ability to act. Ultimately, Rosmer and Rebecca are united in paralysing self-doubt, and the conviction that they must atone for past crimes with their lives. Prompted by Ulrik Brendel's counsel of despair, in what is perhaps the most challenging scene in the play, Rosmer's chilling suggestion that only through Rebecca's sacrifice will he recover his faith, rapidly escalates to become a suicide pact. 'There's no judge to judge us, we must judge ourselves', declares Rosmer, but while in one sense they die to carry out that judgment, in another they solemnize, in the most final way imaginable, their 'marriage', at the same time cancelling their debt of blood to Beata.

Rosmersholm is thus the tragedy of both Rosmer and Rebecca, accelerating with great force as one revelation succeeds another, in this most concentrated of Ibsen's plays. However, the fateful path to the mill-race is very far from straight, weaving in and out of consciousness and memory, constantly being re-routed as incident and character are defined for us not only by their own words and actions, but by the partial judgments passed on them by others, in a tangled cat's-cradle of relationships. On the surface, Ibsen's themes are powerful enough – suicide, incest, conspiracy to murder – but the real drama is played out beneath the surface, in a far murkier world, one which Freud first explored in his *Interpretation of Dreams*, published at the very end of the century, some fourteen years after *Rosmersholm*.

Rosmersholm in Performance

Premièred in Bergen on 17 January 1887, *Rosmersholm* reached Kristiania only in April, and its two-week run in the capital must be accounted a relative failure. The play fared no better in Copenhagen, where it was rejected by the prestige Royal Theatre, and its early years in general were beset by censorship problems, audience incomprehension, and some of the most hostile criticism directed at any of Ibsen's plays. Its London première, for example, at the Vaudeville Theatre on 23 February 1891 was described as 'studies in insanity best fitted for the lecture room at Bedlam' (*The Stage*) and 'brainsick extravagancies' (*Daily News*), although in fairness, a number of more sympathetic reviews appeared to confirm the judgment of the *Daily Chronicle*, that Ibsen's plays 'may have the odour of the *fleurs du mal*, but they are undeniably taking root in English contemporary thought.'

Rosmersholm presents an especially difficult challenge to performers, who must interpret their roles not only as freestanding characters, but also as points of convergence, so to speak, at which several complex, and often conflicting views are made flesh. Ibsen's own advice to the actress Sofie Reimers, who played Rebecca in the first Kristiania production, was that what the other characters had to say about her was at least as important as her own part. This of course raises the question of how reliable those witnesses are, for performers and audience alike. Even more demanding, *Rosmersholm*'s unspoken drama, that denied or forgotten past which colours every relationship, must be carried across the footlights like a charge of electricity. Without that, a work variously described as a masterpiece of construction, and Ibsen's most inexhaustible play, may suffer through its very concentration.

Perhaps because of its perceived difficulty, *Rosmersholm* is
something of a rarity on stage among Ibsen's major works,
and a reviewer of a recent American production, for
example, observed that there have been barely a dozen
stagings of *Rosmersholm* in New York in the past hundred
years. Over that period, notable events include Lugné-Poë's
1893 Paris production at the Théâtre de l'Oeuvre, later
toured to London, where George Bernard Shaw, writing in
the *Saturday Review*, was impressed by the 'true atmosphere
of this most enthralling of all Ibsen's works rising like an
enchanted mist for the first time on an English stage.'
The German impresario Max Reinhardt directed a major
production of *Rosmersholm* in Berlin in 1905, and in 1906
Edward Gordon Craig designed and directed an Italian
production with the great Eleanora Duse. Two years later,
in 1908, Nemirovich-Danchenko introduced the Moscow
Art Theatre to the play, virtually a model demonstration of
the Stanislavsky 'method', with its all-important sub-text.

Following its 1891 British première at the Vaudeville,
Rosmersholm has been seen rather infrequently in the UK,
but stagings of note have taken place at the Kingsway
Theatre (1926), with Edith Evans and Charles Carson; the
Festival Theatre, Cambridge, with Flora Robson and Robert
Donat, directed by Tyrone Guthrie; the Criterion (1936),
with Jean Forbes-Roberston and John Laurie; the Arts
Theatre (1948), with Lucie Mannheim and Marius Goring,
a production also heard on BBC Radio; the Royal Court
(1959) with Peggy Ashcroft and Eric Porter; the Greenwich
Theatre (1973), with Joan Plowright and Jeremy Brett; the
Haymarket (1977) with Claire Bloom; and the National
Theatre (1987), in Frank McGuinness' adaptation, with
Rupert Frazer. In addition to the production already men-
tioned, *Rosmersholm* has had several airings on BBC Radio,
the most recent in 1990, in an adaptation by David Rudkin.

For Further Reading

In addition to a valuable introduction to *Rosmersholm*,
Volume VI of the Oxford *Ibsen*, ed. James McFarlane,
Oxford University Press, 1960, contains an appendix of
Ibsen's early drafts of the play. Edited by the same author,
The Cambridge Companion to Ibsen, Cambridge University
Press, 1994, is a varied collection of essays by a
distinguished international cast, while George B. Bryan's
An Ibsen Companion, Greenwood Press, Westport, Conn.,
1984, is a very useful guide, in dictionary format, to Ibsen's
life and work. A similar function is served by Michael
Meyer's compact little *Ibsen on File*, Methuen, 1985. Meyer's
three-volume *Henrik Ibsen*, revised in 1992, and also
available in a single, condensed volume, is justly regarded
as the authoritative work in English on Ibsen's life, and the
theatre and politics of his day. The pioneer endeavours of
William Archer in bringing Ibsen to the attention of the
English-speaking world, are commemorated in *William
Archer on Ibsen: The Major Essays 1889-1919*, ed. Thomas
Postlethwaite, Greenwood Press, Westport, Conn., 1984,
and P.F.D. Tennant's *Ibsen's Dramatic Technique*, Bowes &
Bowes, Cambridge, 1948, is a persuasive critical analysis
of the major plays. The revised version of Halvdan Koht's
Life of Ibsen, translated by Haugen and Santaniello, and
published by Benjamin Blom, Inc., New York, 1971, despite
its venerable age (first published in 1928 to mark Ibsen's
centennial) is also worth reading, while Robert Ferguson's
Henrik Ibsen – A New Biography, Richard Cohen Books, 1996,

is a fascinating warts-and-all portrayal of a deeply troubled spirit. Finally, Michael Goldman's *Ibsen: The Dramaturgy of Fear*, Columbia University Press, New York, 1999, is a perceptive contribution to Ibsen scholarship.

Ibsen: Key Dates

1828   Born 20 March in Skien, south-east Norway.

1835   Father's business fails, family moves to Venstøp.

1844   Ibsen leaves school, becomes apprentice pharmacist in Grimstad.

1846   Aged eighteen, Ibsen fathers illegitimate son by housemaid Else Sofie Jensdatter.

1849   First play, *Catiline*, rejected by Kristiania Danish Theatre.

1850   Fails university entrance exam. Première of *The Warrior's Barrow*, 26 September, Kristiania Theatre.

1851   Appointed writer-in-residence at Bergen Norwegian Theatre.

1853   *St. John's Night*.

1854   *The Warrior's Barrow* revised.

1855   *Lady Inger of Østråt*.

1856   *The Feast at Solhaug*.

1857   Final contracted play for Bergen Theatre, *Olaf Liljekrans*. Appointed artistic director at Norwegian Theatre in Kristiania.

1858   Marries Suzannah Thoresen, 18 June. *The Vikings at Helgeland*, 24 November.

1862   Norwegian Theatre fails, Ibsen tours Western Norway, collecting folklore.

1864   *The Pretenders*, 17 January, at Kristiania Theatre.

1864   Leaves Norway, travels to Rome, via Copenhagen, Lübeck, Berlin and Vienna.

1866   *Brand*.

1867   *Peer Gynt.*

1868   Moves from Rome to settle in Dresden.

1869   Invited to represent Norway at opening of Suez Canal. *The League of Youth.*

1871   Publication of collected poems.

1873   *Emperor and Galilean.* Première of *Love's Comedy*, Kristiania, 24 November.

1874   Edvard Grieg invited to supply incidental music for *Peer Gynt.*

1875   Leaves Dresden to settle in Munich.

1876   *Peer Gynt* premièred, Kristiania, 24 February.

1877   *Pillars of the Community.*

1879   *A Doll's House.*

1881   *Ghosts.*

1882   *An Enemy of the People.*

1884   *The Wild Duck.*

1886   *Rosmersholm.*

1887   Meininger Company presents *Ghosts*, 23 December.

1888   *The Lady from the Sea.*

1890   Antoine's Théâtre Libre presents *Ghosts*, Paris, 29 May. *Hedda Gabler.*

1891   Returns to Norway, settles in Kristiania.

1892   *The Master Builder.*

1894   *Little Eyolf.*

1896   *John Gabriel Borkman.*

1899   *Hedda Gabler* produced at Moscow Art Theatre. *When We Dead Awaken.*

1900   Suffers first of a series of strokes, 15 March.

1906   Dies 23 May, Kristiania.

ROSMERSHOLM

Characters

JOHANNES ROSMER, *formerly the parish pastor, owner of Rosmersholm*

REBECCA WEST, *who lives at Rosmersholm [originally employed as companion to Rosmer's late wife; now living on in the house in an undefined position (translator's note)].*

LARS KROLL, *a headmaster, Rosmer's brother-in-law*

ULRIK BRENDEL

PEDER MORTENSGÅRD

MRS HELSETH, *Rosmer's housekeeper*

For a Guide to Pronunciation of Names, see p. 100

The action takes place in Rosmersholm, an old manor-house near a small coastal village in West Norway.

ACT ONE

Large sitting-room in Rosmersholm, old-fashioned and comfortable. The walls are covered with portraits, old and new, of clergymen, army officers and government officials in uniform. Down right, stove trimmed with fresh birch-twigs and wild flowers. Beside it, sofa, easy chairs and table. Upstage right, door. Centre back, double doors to the hall. Left, window, in front of which is a stand covered with flowers and house-plants. The window is open. So are the double doors and the outer door beyond; through them we can see an avenue of mature trees leading to the garden.

It is a summer evening, just after sunset. REBECCA WEST *is sitting in a chair by the window, crocheting a large white shawl which she has nearly finished. From time to time she looks out of the window through the plants. After a moment, enter* MRS HELSETH.

MRS HELSETH. It's getting late, Miss. I ought to lay the table?

REBECCA. Yes, please. Mr Rosmer won't be long.

MRS HELSETH. Aren't you in a draught there, Miss?

REBECCA. A little. Please, if you'd –

MRS HELSETH closes the doors to the hall, then returns to the window to close it.

MRS HELSETH *(looking out).* He's coming, now.

REBECCA *(starting).* Where?

She gets up to look, keeping behind the curtain.

Keep back. Don't let him see us.

MRS HELSETH. Look, Miss. He *is* using the old path again. The one by the mill.

REBECCA. Just like the day before yesterday.

She peeps out between the curtain and the window-frame.

Now, will he or won't he – ?

MRS HELSETH. Use the foot-bridge?

REBECCA. That's what I want to see. (*Pause.*) No. He's turning. The other way again. (*Coming from the window.*) The long way round.

MRS HELSETH. I'm not surprised. That bridge . . . after what happened . . . if he never sets foot on it again.

REBECCA (*folding the shawl*). They cling to their dead, at Rosmersholm.

MRS HELSETH. Or the dead cling to Rosmersholm.

REBECCA. What d'you mean?

MRS HELSETH. As if they can't tear themselves away.

REBECCA. What makes you think that?

MRS HELSETH. Well, the White Horse, Miss.

REBECCA. What White Horse?

MRS HELSETH. I know you don't believe in that sort of thing.

REBECCA. Do *you?*

MRS HELSETH (*closing the window*). You'll just make fun of me. (*Looking out.*) Look. There on the mill-path. Has the Pastor changed his mind?

REBECCA (*looking out*). No, that's Doctor Kroll.

MRS HELSETH. Headmaster Kroll.

REBECCA. He's coming to see us.

MRS HELSETH. Straight over the bridge. Even though she *was* his sister. I'd better lay the table, Miss.

Exit right. REBECCA *stands at the window. She smiles and waves. Then she goes to the door, right.*

REBECCA. Mrs Helseth, what about a little treat for dinner? You know what the Headmaster likes.

MRS HELSETH (*off*). I'll find something, Miss.

REBECCA *opens the doors to the hall.*

REBECCA. Doctor Kroll. After all this time. It's wonderful to see you.

KROLL (*in the hall, putting down his walking stick*). My dear Miss West. I'm not disturbing you?

REBECCA. Don't be silly.

KROLL (*coming in*). Thank you.

He looks round.

Is Johannes in his study?

REBECCA. He went for a walk. Further than he expected. He won't be long.

She gestures to him to sit on the sofa.

Please, sit down.

KROLL (*putting down his hat and sitting*). Thank you. My, you have brightened up in here. This stuffy old room. Flowers, everywhere!

REBECCA. Mr Rosmer loves to have fresh flowers, growing plants, all round him.

KROLL. And so do you, I imagine.

REBECCA. They fill a room with perfume. And till recently, we had to do without.

KROLL. Poor Beata. The scent was too much for her.

REBECCA. The colours made her head spin.

KROLL. Yes. Yes. (*More cheerfully.*) Well, how are you all, so far from town?

REBECCA. Quiet. The same as usual. One day much like another. And you . . . ? Mrs Kroll . . . ?

KROLL. Dear Miss West, don't let's talk about me. Family life . . . there's always something. These days, especially.

Pause. REBECCA *sits in an armchair beside the sofa.*

REBECCA. The holidays'll be over soon. You'll be back at school. Why haven't you been to see us, in all that time?

KROLL. Didn't want to impose.

REBECCA. You know how we've missed you.

KROLL. And I was away, of course.

REBECCA. Two weeks, that's right. I suppose it was politics.

KROLL. Who'd have guessed it? Headmaster Kroll, in his doddering old age, manning the barricades.

REBECCA (*lightly*). Oh, you've always been a hothead.

KROLL. In a quiet way. But now it's serious. D'you read the radical papers?

REBECCA. I can't deny I –

KROLL. Dear Miss West, it's harmless. At least, for you.

REBECCA. We have to keep up –

KROLL. It's not as if you were expected to take *sides*. A woman! But it's a civil war. You must have seen what the 'champions of the people' have been saying, the way they've been treating me. Impertinence!

REBECCA. I think you gave as good as you got.

KROLL. I flatter myself I've tasted blood. They'll find I'm not a man who'll let himself be – (*breaking off*) I'm sorry. Let's change the subject. It's so *annoying*.

REBECCA. Let's change the subject.

KROLL. How are things here for you at Rosmersholm, now that you're on your own. Now that poor Beata's –

REBECCA. Fine, thank you. There's a huge gap, naturally. Sorrow, mourning. But otherwise . . .

KROLL. Are you planning to stay? For good, I mean.

REBECCA. Dear Doctor Kroll, I haven't thought about it, one way or the other. I'm so used to Rosmersholm, it's as if I belonged here.

KROLL. Of course you do.

REBECCA. So long as Mr Rosmer finds me useful, a comfort . . . well, I'll stay.

KROLL (*looking at her with admiration*). You know, when a woman sacrifices her life for others, it's wonderful.

REBECCA. My life. What else was I to do with it?

KROLL. All those years with that impossible man, your foster-father in his wheelchair.

REBECCA. Doctor West was fine up north in Finmark. It was the boat-journeys he couldn't stand. Then, when we moved south, until he died, we did have two or three bad years.

KROLL. Not so bad as what happened afterwards.

REBECCA. How can you say that? Poor Beata. I was fond of her. She needed me, my care, my company . . .

KROLL (*warmly*). Thank you for remembering her so kindly.

REBECCA (*going to him*). Doctor Kroll, you mean that. You're *not* irritated.

KROLL. What d'you mean?

REBECCA. It wouldn't be surprising. A stranger, here, in Rosmersholm, running things.

KROLL. You're joking.

REBECCA. You *don't* mind! (*Taking his hand.*) Doctor Kroll, oh thank you.

KROLL. Whatever made you think I was irritated?

REBECCA. When you didn't call . . .

KROLL. My dear, you were quite mistaken. In any case, nothing's changed. When Beata was alive, you still had to —

REBECCA. That was different. Like a regent, ruling in the lady's name.

KROLL. Whatever you say. Dear Miss West, I wouldn't even mind if you — No. None of my business.

REBECCA. What isn't?

KROLL. If it . . . if things . . . if one day you . . . I mean, the empty place . . .

REBECCA. Doctor Kroll, I've all the place I want.

KROLL. Well, yes. But I meant —

REBECCA (*interrupting him, gravely*). Headmaster, how can you joke about such matters? Tut!

KROLL. Well, Johannes probably thinks he's had enough of marriage. But it *could* be –

REBECCA. It's absurd.

KROLL. If you say so. Miss West, if you'll pardon me asking . . . How old are you?

REBECCA. Embarrassingly, I'm twenty-nine, Headmaster. In my thirtieth year already.

KROLL. And Johannes is . . . Hum. Five years younger than me. Forty-three. It would be perfectly in order.

REBECCA. Who could possibly object? (*Getting up.*) Will you stay to supper?

KROLL. Thank you. I wanted to stay. I need to talk to Johannes. In any case, dear Miss West, I'd better start coming far more often, in case you think I'm *irritated* again.

REBECCA. Of course you must. (*Taking his hands.*) You're *such* a nice man!

KROLL. Oh, hum, you should hear what they say at home.

Enter ROSMER *right.*

REBECCA. Mr Rosmer, look who's here!

ROSMER. Mrs Helseth told me.

KROLL *has stood up.* ROSMER *takes his hands warmly.*

Welcome, Lars, you're welcome. Dear old friend, I was sure one day it'd be all right again.

KROLL. You too? You thought as well – ?

REBECCA (*to* ROSMER). You won't believe it – We imagined the whole thing,

ROSMER. But Lars, you stayed away entirely.

KROLL. If I'd come you'd have been reminded . . . all those years of misery . . . the one who . . . ended in the millrace.

ROSMER. Considerate as always! But there was no need. Really. Come and sit down.

They sit on the sofa.

I promise you, I'm not upset when I think about Beata. We talk about her always. It's as if we had her still here, still one of us.

KROLL. You feel that really?

REBECCA (*lighting the lamp*). Both of us.

ROSMER. It's hardly surprising. We were so fond of her. And we feel, Rebec – Miss West and I, both of us, that we did all we could. The way she was, poor soul. We've nothing to be ashamed of. When I think about Beata now, it's tenderly, warmly . . .

KROLL. How kind you both are. From now on, I'll visit every day.

REBECCA (*sitting in an armchair*). We'll insist on it.

ROSMER (*with some awkwardness*). Lars . . . I was so sorry when I . . . when we . . . I mean, all these years we've known each other. You've been my guide, my friend . . . ever since I was a student.

KROLL. And I've been proud to be so. Is there something now, especially . . . ?

ROSMER. Yes. Something important. We need to talk about it.

REBECCA. That's right, Mr Rosmer, what could be better? A talk with an old, dear friend.

KROLL. Johannes, I've been meaning to . . . for some time . . . You know I'm involved in politics?

ROSMER. Yes. How on earth did that happen?

KROLL. No choice. Absolutely none. I couldn't stand by any longer. The radicals in power . . . a tragedy, I had to do something. I've persuaded our little local group to close ranks. I had to do something.

REBECCA (*smiling slightly*). You may just be a little late.

KROLL. It *would* have been better earlier. Divert the stream before it becomes a torrent . . . But who could have guessed – ? (*Pacing.*) I mean, they've even infiltrated College.

ROSMER. Your school? You're joking.

KROLL. I mean it. College. I discovered that the sixth form – or some of them, at least – started a secret society six months ago. They've been buying that rag of Mortensgård's.

REBECCA. 'The Searchlight'.

KROLL. What sort of reading is that for future civil servants? Now – it's unbelievable – some of the brighter ones are agitating against me. Not the dunces, oh not the dunces.

REBECCA. You really think it matters?

KROLL. Matters? To be hampered, blocked, in everything I stand for. (*Lower.*) It's not just College. I could cope with that. It's worse. (*Looking all round.*) We are alone?

REBECCA. There's no one.

KROLL. Then I'll tell you. Revolt, opposition . . . in my own family. My sanctuary, my haven.

ROSMER. What d'you mean?

REBECCA. Doctor Kroll, what's happened?

KROLL. To think that my own children would . . . Oh: this group in College, Lauritz is the ring-leader. And Hilda's made a cover to keep that 'Searchlight' in –
a red one.

ROSMER. Unbelievable . . . Your own family . . .

KROLL. My family. A haven of discipline, obedience. One person's will, his guiding hand –

REBECCA. What does your wife make of it all?

KROLL. That's the part I find hardest to believe. All her life she's agreed with me, big things, small things – and now she's taken it into her head to side with the children. It's all my fault, she says. I treat them like a tyrant. How else is a father to – ? Well, revolt, opposition, the bosom of the family . . . I don't talk about it. It's private. (*Pacing.*) Well. Well.

He stands looking out of the window. REBECCA *says urgently to* ROSMER, *so that* KROLL *can't hear her:*

REBECCA. Do it now.

ROSMER. Not tonight.

REBECCA. Tonight.

KROLL *turns, and she goes and adjusts the lamp.*

KROLL (*going to* ROSMER). That's it, Johannes. The times we live in. My work, my family life, poisoned. The times we live in. Law and order, trust, good citizenship collapsing all round us. Well, I'm fighting it. Tongue, pen, any weapons I can lay my hands on. Fighting it.

ROSMER. You mean it.

KROLL. My duty, nothing more. And everyone else's, every man who calls himself a patriot, right-minded . . . That's why I'm here this evening.

ROSMER. What? Lars, you don't mean me.

KROLL. Stand by your friends. Stand up and be counted. Do anything you can.

REBECCA. Doctor Kroll, Mr Rosmer hates that kind of thing. You know he does.

KROLL. He'll have to stop hating it. Johannes, you don't know what's going on. You bury yourself out here, nose in your books . . . Family trees! Good Heavens! I'm sorry, but some things are more important. Don't you see what's happening, all over the country? Everything we believed in, everything we stood for, turned upside down. To put things right, to straighten things out again: it'll take every ounce of effort.

ROSMER. Oh, I'm hardly the man to –

REBECCA. Recently Mr Rosmer's begun to see things with clearer eyes.

KROLL (*astounded*). Clearer eyes?

REBECCA. Less blinkered. Less one-sided.

KROLL. What d'you mean? Johannes? Don't tell me you've let yourself . . . ? Just because those loud-mouths have scored a few little victories . . . ?

ROSMER. Lars, you know I know nothing about politics. It's just that, these last few years, people do seem to have started thinking for themselves.

KROLL. And you think that's good? Oh my friend, how wrong you are. What are these new radical thoughts they're thinking for themselves? Out here; in town? I'll tell you: nothing more or less than the word according to 'The Searchlight'.

REBECCA. That's right. Round here, plenty of people agree with Mortensgård.

KROLL. And isn't that amazing? A man with his record! Sacked from teaching for . . . irregular behaviour. Sets himself up as the voice of the people – and they listen! They listen! I heard he's thinking of expanding that rag of his. As soon as he can find a competent assistant.

REBECCA. I'm surprised you and your friends don't start an opposition paper.

KROLL. Oh, we're going to. Today we bought the 'County Telegraph'. No trouble about the funds. The thing is . . . (*Turning to* ROSMER.) The real reason I came . . . The *thrust* of the paper, the editorial *thrust* . . . What I'm saying, Johannes, for the sake of everything we're trying to do, if *you'd* consider –

ROSMER (*taken right aback*). Me?

REBECCA. You don't know what you're asking.

KROLL. I know you hate public meetings – and the people who go to them, I'm not surprised. But an editor's more private, in the background, how shall I put it . . . ?

ROSMER. It's impossible. Don't ask me.

KROLL. I'd do it myself, but I simply haven't time. Too busy. But you, a man of leisure . . . Of course, we'll give you all the help we can.

ROSMER. Lars, I can't. I wouldn't know how.

KROLL. That's exactly what you said when your father found you this parish.

ROSMER. And I was right. Why d'you think I resigned?

KROLL. If you're as good an editor as you were a pastor, we won't be complaining.

ROSMER. For the last time, Lars, I don't accept.

KROLL. All right, at least let us use your name.

ROSMER. My name?

KROLL. Johannes Rosmer: what a coup for the paper! The rest of us, we're activists – I gather some people call me a fanatic. If our names are on the paper, the brainless masses won't touch it. But you've always kept out of the struggle. Everyone knows you, respects you: your decency, high-mindedness, integrity. The fact you were a pastor. Your old family name.

ROSMER. The family name.

KROLL (*pointing to the portraits*). The Rosmers of Rosmersholm. Clergymen, soldiers, respected politicians, gentlemen to their finger-ends, a family people here have looked up to for two hundred years. Johannes, you owe it to yourself, your breeding, your standing, to protect everything that, till recently, has been finest and most sacred in this society of ours. (*To* REBECCA.) Don't you agree, Miss West?

REBECCA. Doctor Kroll, I've never heard anything so silly.

KROLL. Silly!

REBECCA. It's time I told you –

ROSMER (*sharply*). No. Leave it. Not now.

KROLL (*looking from one to the other*). What on earth's going – ? (*Interrupting himself.*) Hum, hum.

Enter MRS HELSETH *right*.

MRS HELSETH. Sir, there's a man at the kitchen door. He says he'd like to see you.

ROSMER (*relieved*). Fine. Bring him in.

MRS HELSETH. In here, sir?

ROSMER. Naturally.

MRS HELSETH. This is not the kind of man you bring into the parlour.

REBECCA. Mrs Helseth! What's wrong with him?

MRS HELSETH. He doesn't look much.

ROSMER. Didn't he say his name?

MRS HELSETH. Hekman, something like that.

ROSMER. I don't know any Hekman.

MRS HELSETH. His other name was Ulrik.

ROSMER (*startled*). Hetman. Ulrik Hetman. Was that it?

MRS HELSETH. Yes, sir. Hetman.

KROLL. Sounds vaguely familiar.

REBECCA. Wasn't it a pen-name, that odd man's pen-name?

ROSMER (*to* KROLL). She means Ulrik Brendel. *His* penname.

KROLL. Ulrik Brendel. That good-for-nothing.

REBECCA. He's still alive.

ROSMER. I heard he'd become an actor.

KROLL. I heard he was in the workhouse.

ROSMER. Ask him in, Mrs Helseth.

MRS HELSETH. If you say so, sir.

Exit.

KROLL. You're inviting him *in*?

ROSMER. My old tutor, of course I am.

KROLL. Cramming your head with revolutionary nonsense, till your father showed him the door – with a horsewhip.

ROSMER (*with a little bitterness*). Even in the family, my father was always the general.

KROLL. And you should go down on your knees to thank his memory. Ha!

MRS HELSETH *shows* ULRIK BRENDEL *in right, then goes and closes the door.* BRENDEL *is a distinguished-looking man with grey hair and beard, gaunt but active. He is dressed as a tramp: shabby frock-coat, worn-out shoes, no shirt. He wears old, black gloves, carries a dirty soft hat under one arm and a walking-stick. He stands a moment, hesitating, then goes and holds out his hand to* KROLL.

BRENDEL. Johannes, dear boy, good evening.

KROLL. Ah, I –

BRENDEL. I know! You never expected to set eyes on me again. In this detested room.

KROLL. Um, I –

He indicates ROSMER.

That's –

BRENDEL (*turning*). Of course. Johannes, dear boy, dear boy . . .

ROSMER (*shaking his hand*). Good to see you, sir.

BRENDEL. Despite all the unhappy memories that came flooding in, flooding, I couldn't pass this house without calling to pay my respects.

ROSMER. You're welcome. Welcome.

BRENDEL. And this charming lady? (*Bowing.*) Mrs Rosmer, one does see that.

ROSMER. Miss West.

BRENDEL. A close relation. One sees that at once. And this gentleman . . . ? A man of the cloth, one does see that.

ROSMER. Headmaster Kroll.

BRENDEL. Kroll . . . Kroll . . . Weren't you . . . years ago . . . didn't you read philology?

KROLL. Certainly.

BRENDEL. *Donnerwetter*, man, our paths have crossed!

KROLL. I'm sorry.

BRENDEL. You were one of the –

KROLL. I'm sorry.

BRENDEL. One of the Brethren of Light who had me *hurled* from the Debating Union.

KROLL. Very likely. But I deny any closer acquaintance.

BRENDEL. Really? *Nach belieben, Herr Doktor*. No matter. I'll survive. One is nothing if not a survivor.

REBECCA. Are you on your way to town, Mr Brendel?

BRENDEL. Nail on the head, dear lady. It happens, now and then, needs must, one is compelled to work. *Infra dig*, one does see that, but, *enfin*, when the Devil drives . . .

ROSMER. My dear Mr Brendel, you must allow me. There must be something –

BRENDEL. Tut tut, dear boy. After all we've been through. Johannes, never!

ROSMER. But what will you do in town? It won't be easy to –

BRENDEL. Leave that to me, dear lad. The die is cast. You see me now, embarked on a journey, nay a campaign, more wide in scope than all previous excursions. (*To* KROLL.) My dear Professor, *unter uns*, is there by any chance, in this fair town of yours, some respectable, clean, commodious public hall?

KROLL. The Mechanics Institute is the biggest.

BRENDEL. And you, most esteemed of pedagogues, no doubt your word is *law* with the committee?

KROLL. I've never even met them.

REBECCA (*to* BRENDEL). The man you want is Peder Mortensgård.

BRENDEL. Ah! One of the *hoi polloi*.

ROSMER. What makes you think so?

BRENDEL. The name, dear boy. Shrieks *hoi polloi*.

KROLL. Well, that was unexpected.

BRENDEL. Still, one must conquer one's distaste. Needs must. When one's standing at the crossroads . . . and one *is* . . . That's settled, then. I'll approach the fellow directly, negotiate directly.

ROSMER. Do you mean that? You're standing at a crossroads?

BRENDEL. Darling boy, don't you remember? Wherever Ulrik Brendel stands, he *stands*. Look your last on me as I was. I'm throwing off this modest demeanour, this cloak of reserve I wear.

ROSMER. What d'you mean?

BRENDEL. I'm taking a firm grip on life, striding forth, my eyes on the stars. The air we breathe is stormy, stormy. I intend to place my offering on the altar of – equality.

KROLL. Not another one.

BRENDEL (*to them all*). Your people here: are they familiar at all with my various writings?

KROLL. I must confess I –

REBECCA. I've read some of them. My foster-father –

BRENDEL. Rubbish, dear lady, rubbish. Take it from me. A waste of your time.

REBECCA. You think so?

BRENDEL. Absolutely. The ones you've read so far. The ones to come, my true *oeuvre*, what man or woman on earth knows anything of that? No one, save only – myself.

REBECCA. Why's that?

BRENDEL. I've still to write them.

ROSMER. My dear Mr Brendel –

BRENDEL. Johannes, dear Johannes, you know me: I've
    always been, one might almost say, a *Feinschmecker*, a
    sybarite. From my earliest youth I was solitary, took
    pleasure in my own company, double pleasure, tenfold.
    When golden dreams swept down on me, engulfed me,
    when new ideas, new dizzying, horizon-stretching thoughts
    were born in me, when I soared aloft on their beating
    wings, I fleshed them in poems, visions, pictures.
    Blueprints, sketches in the mind, you understand –

ROSMER. If you say so.

BRENDEL. Oh the joy I've known, the exhilaration. The
    mysterious rapture of creation – in sketches in the mind –
    the applause, the cheers, the votes of thanks, the laurel
    crowns, I stretched out my trembling hands and grasped
    them all. And then, in my secret thoughts, with what
    rapture, what soaring ecstasy –

KROLL. Ahem.

ROSMER. But you wrote nothing down.

BRENDEL. Not a single word. The scribe, his bending toil,
    I shudder at it, shudder. In any case, why cast my ideas
    abroad when I could enjoy them myself in purity,
    untrammelled? But now it's time to offer them. I feel as
    a mother must feel, when she entrusts her daughter to a
    husband's arms. But still I give them, on the altar of
    equality I offer them. A lecture series, carefully structured,
    all over the country –

REBECCA (*eyes shining*). How brave, Mr Brendel! To give up
    the dearest thing you have.

BRENDEL. The only thing I have.

REBECCA (*looking pointedly at* ROSMER). How many of *us* would do as much? Would *dare* as much?

ROSMER (*returning the look*). Who knows?

BRENDEL. The company is moved. That heartens one's heart and steels one's will. On, then, to action. Stay, there's one thing more. (*To* KROLL.) Mr Pedagogue, is there such as thing as a Temperance Society in town? Total Abstainers? I need hardly ask.

KROLL. Most certainly. I have the honour to be –

BRENDEL. Its chairman. I could tell at a glance. Well, it's not impossible that I may call and inscribe my name, for a week.

KROLL. Unfortunately, we don't have weekly members.

BRENDEL. *À la bonne heure*, Mr Blackboard. On societies of that kind, Ulrik Brendel has never yet imposed himself. (*Turning.*) But I mustn't outstay my welcome, in this house so rich in memories. I must to town, select some suitable place to lay my head. There is a clean hotel, no doubt.

REBECCA. Won't you drink something before you go?

BRENDEL. What kind of something?

REBECCA. A cup of tea –

BRENDEL. My heartfelt thanks, dear, generous lady, but I fear I intrude on a private party. (*With a wave of his hand.*) Adieu, then, one and all.

He goes to the door, then turns back.

Oh, I almost forgot . . . Johannes, dear Johannes, a small favour for your old tutor, for our many years' long friendship?

ROSMER. Whatever I can.

BRENDEL. Thank you. Then lend me, pray – for a day or two – a clean shirt, with cuffs.

ROSMER. Nothing else?

BRENDEL. Thing is, I'm travelling on foot, at present. Shanks' mare. My trunk's on its way, they're sending it on.

ROSMER. Is there nothing else we can help you with?

BRENDEL. D'you know, if by any chance you had an old, *decrepit* summer jacket . . .

ROSMER. I think I can find one.

BRENDEL. And a pair of boots to go with it?

ROSMER. As soon as we know your address, we'll send them on.

BRENDEL. I won't hear of it! Such trouble, for my sake! Give me the trifles, I'll carry them myself.

ROSMER. Come upstairs: we'll have a look.

REBECCA. Let me go. Mrs Helseth and I will see to it.

BRENDEL. A lady of rank! I wouldn't *dream* –

REBECCA. Mr Brendel, don't be silly. This way.

Exit right. BRENDEL *makes to follow her, but* ROSMER *stops him.*

ROSMER. Are you sure there's nothing else I can do?

BRENDEL. Can't think of a thing. No, damn it, that reminds me . . . Johannes, do you happen to have eight kroner in cash?

ROSMER. I'll have a look.

He takes out his wallet.

Two ten-kroner notes.

BRENDEL. No matter, I'll take them. I can change them in town. Thank you. Remember: two tenners I owe you. Now, darling boy, good evening. And Your Reverence, good evening.

Exit right. ROSMER *goes to say goodbye, and closes the door after him.*

KROLL. Merciful Heaven, so that's Ulrik Brendel. After all that promise!

ROSMER (*quietly*). At least he has the courage to *choose* the way he lives. Not a little thing.

KROLL. You're joking. A life like that? I think he could *still* fill your head with craziness.

ROSMER. Oh no. My mind's made up. My path is set.

KROLL. Johannes, I wish I believed it.

ROSMER. Sit down with me. I want to ask you something.

KROLL. By all means.

They sit on the sofa. Pause.

ROSMER. What d'you think of our life at Rosmersholm? Pleasant, comfortable . . . ?

KROLL. Pleasant, comfortable, at ease. You've a happy home, Johannes. And I've lost mine.

ROSMER. Don't say that. Problems at the moment, but they won't last forever.

KROLL. The sting can't be drawn. Nothing'll be the same again.

ROSMER. Lars, I want to ask you . . . We've been friends all these years . . . D'you think anything could come between us?

KROLL. Nothing I can think of. What's put that into your head?

ROSMER. You think it's so vital that everyone shares the same views, the same ideals.

KROLL. Well, naturally. But we see eye to eye on most things, most important things.

ROSMER (*quietly*). Not any longer.

KROLL. What d'you mean?

ROSMER. No, stay. Please, Lars.

KROLL. What's going on? I don't understand. Tell me.

ROSMER. Summer's bloomed for me again. My eyes are young again. I'm standing . . .

KROLL. Where are you standing?

ROSMER. Where your children stand.

KROLL. You? You can't mean it.

ROSMER. Where Lauritz and Hilda stand.

KROLL. A traitor. Johannes Rosmer, a traitor.

ROSMER. I should be happy. In my treachery, what you call my treachery, so happy. But it's agony. I knew you'd be so wounded.

KROLL. Johannes, Johannes, I'll never forgive you. (*Looking heavily at him.*) How can you – you! – agree with, work for, the forces of ruin in our benighted country?

ROSMER. I want to help with equality.

KROLL. Equality! That's what they call it, the rabble-rousers and the people they're deluding. Listen to me: when our whole society has been poisoned, how can there be equality?

ROSMER. I don't like the rabble-rousers, or the mood they inspire. I want to try to unite people, from all sides. As many as possible. Unite them. I want to devote my life, my strength, to it: the fight for true equality.

KROLL. Don't you think we've all the equality we need? What d'you want? Are we all to be dragged into the gutter, where only the rabble used to thrive?

ROSMER. That's the whole point. That's what I'm fighting for.

KROLL. What, exactly?

ROSMER. To make all our citizens princes.

KROLL. All of them?

ROSMER. As many as possible.

KROLL. And how, precisely?

ROSMER. By setting free their minds, their wills.

KROLL. You're dreaming. Who's going to free them, their minds, their wills – you, personally?

ROSMER. Of course not, Lars. All I can do is show the way. The doing is up to them.

KROLL. You think they can?

ROSMER. Oh yes.

KROLL. With no one to help them?

ROSMER. By their own power, yes.

KROLL (*getting up*). Is this how pastors talk?

ROSMER. I gave up being a pastor.

KROLL. The faith of your fathers?

ROSMER. I've lost it.

KROLL. Lost it!

ROSMER (*getting up*). Surrendered it. I had to, Lars.

KROLL (*fighting emotion*). H'm. H'm. Yes. One thing leads to the other. Is that why you gave up the pastorship?

ROSMER. Yes. When I was knew it wasn't a passing temptation, that it was certainty, something I couldn't, wouldn't shake myself out of – then I left the church.

KROLL. So it's been a long time in your mind. And none of us, none of your friends, had the slightest idea. Johannes, this is a dismal thing. Why didn't you tell us?

ROSMER. I thought *I* had to deal with it, no one else. I didn't want to hurt you unnecessarily, you and my other friends. I thought I could go on here just as before. Calmly, contentedly. I wanted to study, to lose myself in all the subjects that were still closed books to me. To discover the enormous world of truth and freedom that was suddenly opened up to me.

KROLL. A traitor. You prove it with every word you utter. But why admit it? Why not keep it a secret? And why admit it now?

ROSMER. Lars, you left me no choice.

KROLL. *I* left you no choice?

ROSMER. When I heard how you ranted at meetings, when I read the speeches you made, the way you attacked and sneered at anyone who disagreed – oh Lars, to think this was *you* doing this! – you left me no choice. There's a kind of war going on, people are suffering, we should be working for peace and happiness and reconciliation. That's why I'm speaking out now, proclaiming what I believe. I must do all I can. Lars, help me – I know we disagree, but help me.

KROLL. There are forces tearing society apart, and you want me to help them? I won't.

ROSMER. Then if we have to fight, at least let's fight with honour.

KROLL. In this particular struggle, for survival, if a man's not with me he's against me. I reject him. Nothing more to do with him.

ROSMER. You mean me?

KROLL. Johannes, you made the break.

ROSMER. There isn't a break.

KROLL. There is. From everyone you've ever known. You must live with what you've done.

REBECCA *comes in right, opening the door wide.*

REBECCA. There. He's off to make his sacrifice, and we can go in to dinner. Doctor Kroll, this way.

KROLL (*taking his hat*). This is no place for me, Miss West. Goodnight.

REBECCA (*eagerly*). What's happened?

She shuts the door and comes further in.

You've told him?

ROSMER. Now he knows.

KROLL. We won't let you go, Johannes. We'll make sure that you come back.

ROSMER. Not where I was before.

KROLL. You're not a man to stand alone.

ROSMER. As to that . . . there are two of us, here alone.

KROLL. Aha. (*Suddenly.*) That's what Beata –

ROSMER. What, Beata – ?

KROLL (*putting it aside*). No. Unforgivable. I'm sorry.

ROSMER. What are you talking about?

KROLL. Never mind. Nothing. I'm sorry. Goodbye.

He goes to the hall door. ROSMER *follows him.*

ROSMER. Lars! We can't leave it like this. I'll come round tomorrow.

KROLL (*in the hall, turning to face him*). You won't be welcome.

He takes his stick and exits. ROSMER *stands awhile, then comes into the room and shuts the door. He comes down to the table.*

ROSMER. Rebecca, it's nothing. We'll weather it, true comrades in arms. The two of us. Darling.*

REBECCA. What did he mean, 'Unforgivable'?

ROSMER. Oh my dear, it doesn't matter. He didn't mean it. I'll go round tomorrow. Goodnight.

REBECCA. You're going up early? After what's happened?

---

* *Translator's note:* from now on, when alone, they use 'du' to one another: between an unmarried man and woman, a sign of intimacy. Ibsen places it here for maximum impact on the audience.

ROSMER. No different from usual. I'm so relieved now it's over. Look, my dear, I'm calm. You, too, be calm. Goodnight.

REBECCA. Goodnight, my dear. Sleep well.

ROSMER *goes out through the hall door. We hear his steps going up the stairs.* REBECCA *goes to the bell-pull by the stove, and rings. After a moment, enter* MRS HELSETH *right.*

No supper after all, Mrs Helseth. The pastor isn't hungry, and Doctor Kroll went home.

MRS HELSETH. Went home, Miss? Was anything the matter?

REBECCA (*unfolding her crochet-work*). He said a storm was brewing.

MRS HELSETH. But there isn't a cloud in the sky.

REBECCA. Let's hope he doesn't meet the White Horse. I think ghosts'll be stirring soon.

MRS HELSETH. God save us, Miss, don't say such things.

REBECCA. Just joking.

MRS HELSETH. D'you really think, Miss, that someone's time is near?

REBECCA. Of course I don't. The world's full of white horses, Mrs Helseth. They're everywhere. Well, I'm going to bed. Goodnight.

MRS HELSETH. Goodnight, Miss.

Exit REBECCA *right, with her crochet-work.* MRS HELSETH *turns down the lamp, shaking her head and muttering.*

Lord, that young lady. The things she says.

End of Act One.

ACT TWO

ROSMER's *study. Left, entrance door, old-fashioned sofa and table. Centre, a curtained doorway leading to his bedroom. (The curtain is drawn back.) Right, in front of the window, a writing-table covered with books and papers. Bookshelves, cupboards. The furniture is plain and Spartan.*

ROSMER, *in smoking-jacket, is sitting in a high-backed chair at his writing-table, cutting the pages of a journal and stopping occasionally to read. Knock at the door.*

ROSMER (*without turning*). Come in.

Enter REBECCA, *in a housecoat.*

REBECCA. Good morning.

ROSMER (*still busy with his journal*). Good morning, my dear. Did you want something?

REBECCA. Just to see if you slept well.

ROSMER. Soundly, peacefully, not a single dream. (*Turning.*) What about you?

REBECCA. Yes, thank you. Once I *got* to sleep.

ROSMER. I don't know when I've felt so relieved. Thank goodness the chance came to tell him.

REBECCA. Johannes, you shouldn't have kept quiet so long.

ROSMER. I can't think why I was such a coward.

REBECCA. Not cowardice –

ROSMER. Yes, my dear. If I'm honest, it was cowardice.

REBECCA. All the braver of you to face it.

She sits in a chair beside him at the writing-table.

I've something to tell you. Something I did. You mustn't be angry.

ROSMER. My dear: why should I be angry?

REBECCA. I should have asked you first.

ROSMER. What is it?

REBECCA. Last night, when Ulrik Brendel was leaving, I wrote him a note to Mortensgård.

ROSMER (*taken aback*). My dear Rebecca. What did you write?

REBECCA. That he'd be doing you a favour if he helped the poor man, whatever way he could.

ROSMER. My dear, you shouldn't have. This won't help Brendel. And Mortensgård's a man I particularly don't want to get involved with. After what happened before between us.

REBECCA. Don't you think it might be a good idea to make contact again?

ROSMER. Whatever for?

REBECCA. The way things are . . . this break with your old friends . . .

ROSMER (*looking at her, shaking his head*). You really think Kroll, or any of the others, would . . . that they'd bring themselves to − ?

REBECCA. In the heat of anger. My dear, who can tell? The way Kroll took it yesterday . . .

ROSMER. You know Kroll better than that. Whatever else, he is a gentleman. I'll go into town this afternoon, talk to him, talk to them all. It'll be all right. It *will*.

MRS HELSETH comes to the door. REBECCA gets up.

REBECCA. Yes, Mrs Helseth?

MRS HELSETH. Sir, Doctor Kroll's downstairs.

ROSMER (*getting up*). Kroll's here!

REBECCA. Amazing.

MRS HELSETH. He'd like to speak to Pastor Rosmer.

ROSMER (*to* REBECCA). I told you! Of course he can.

He goes to the door and calls:

My dear fellow, come in, come in. Delighted to see you.

He holds open the door. MRS HELSETH *goes.* REBECCA *draws the curtain over the bedroom door, and fusses with this and that. Enter* KROLL, *hat in hand.* ROSMER *speaks with emotion.*

I knew that wouldn't be the end of it.

KROLL. This morning I see the whole thing in an entirely different light.

ROSMER. I told you, Lars. I said you would. When you'd had time to think –

KROLL. That's not what I meant at all.

He puts his hat on the table by the sofa.

I have to speak to you, alone.

ROSMER. There's no reason why Miss West –

REBECCA. It's all right, Pastor Rosmer. I'll leave you alone.

KROLL (*looking her up and down*). And I really must apologise
for calling so early in the day, surprising you before you've
had time to –

REBECCA (*taken aback*). What d'you mean? It's wrong for me
to wear a housecoat about the house?

KROLL. Absolutely not. In any case, these days it's none of
my business what's right or wrong at Rosmersholm.

ROSMER. Lars, what's wrong with you today?

REBECCA. Doctor Kroll, if you'll excuse me.

Exit.

KROLL. Now, if I may –

He sits on the sofa.

ROSMER. Yes, let's sit and talk like friends.

He sits in a chair, facing KROLL.

KROLL. I haven't slept a wink since yesterday. All night I've
been lying and thinking.

ROSMER. And what are your conclusions?

KROLL. Johannes, it'll take some time to explain. First of all,
a kind of preface. Something about Ulrik Brendel.

ROSMER. He called on you?

KROLL. He set himself up in some gutter pub. With gutter
company. Drinking, buying drinks all round so long as the
money lasted. Then he began calling them names, saying
they were lowest of the low – which of course they were –
until finally they beat him up and threw him out.

ROSMER. He hasn't changed, then.

KROLL. He'd also pawned the coat. But someone redeemed it for him. Guess who.

ROSMER. Your good self?

KROLL. Your Mr Mortensgård.

ROSMER. I see.

KROLL. I gather the first person Mr Brendel went to see was that 'man of the people', that 'egalitarian'.

ROSMER. Just as well he did.

KROLL. Exactly.

He leans closer.

Which brings me to the point. I've come to warn you. As an old friend – a former friend. To warn you.

ROSMER. Lars, what is it?

KROLL. There are things going on, here in this house, behind your back.

ROSMER. You don't mean Reb – Miss West?

KROLL. Precisely. I'm not blaming her. She's had her own way here so long. But still I –

ROSMER. Lars, you're completely mistaken. Miss West and I, we have absolutely no secrets from each other. In anything.

KROLL. So she's told you she's been writing to the editor of the 'Searchlight'?

ROSMER. You mean the note she gave Ulrik Brendel?

KROLL. You *do* know. And do you approve? She makes contact with that hack, who never lets a week go by without pillorying me, as a teacher, a private individual –

ROSMER. Lars, it probably never even crossed her mind. Besides, she's a free agent, an entirely free agent. We both are.

KROLL. Is she now? This new philosophy of yours. Presumably she shares it?

ROSMER. We've made progress together, faithful companions.

KROLL. You're blind. You're completely blind.

ROSMER. What d'you mean?

KROLL. I can't – won't – believe the alternative. Let me finish. Johannes, you really value my friendship, my respect. Don't you?

ROSMER. You surely don't want me to answer that.

KROLL. Other questions must be answered. Clearly, honestly. If you'll allow me . . .

ROSMER. An interrogation?

KROLL. Some things you may find painful, you may prefer to have forgotten. This betrayal of yours, equality you call it – other things are involved, all kinds of other things. I want you to explain.

ROSMER. My dear Lars, ask anything you like. I've nothing to hide.

KROLL. Very well. What d'you think the real reason was, the real reason, for Beata's suicide?

ROSMER. You think there's some doubt? I mean, she was sick, unhappy, not responsible for her actions –

KROLL. Not responsible? You're sure of that? The doctors didn't think so.

ROSMER. If they'd seen her as I saw her, the days, the nights, they'd have thought so.

KROLL. I certainly thought so – at the time.

ROSMER. No doubt about it. I told you what she was like: insane, headlong passion . . . she tried to make me respond, it was appalling . . . then the last years, when she blamed herself, no reason, when she tormented herself with guilt . . .

KROLL. Because she couldn't have children.

ROSMER. To rack yourself like that, for something you couldn't control! Responsible for her actions . . . !

KROLL. I wonder . . . Can you remember . . . ? Were there books lying about the house at the time . . . the responsibilities of marriage . . . advanced ideas . . . ?

ROSMER. Miss West lent me something of the kind. From her foster-father's library. Lars, for Heaven's sake, you don't imagine we let Beata find such a thing? In her condition! I swear to you, we'd nothing to do with it. Her own state of mind brought on her fits.

KROLL. I do know one thing: that tormented, neurotic woman killed herself so that you'd have the chance to live happily, freely – any way you wanted.

ROSMER. What are you talking about?

KROLL. Listen to what I'm saying, Johannes. It's time to tell you. In the last year of her life, she came to me twice, to pour out her misery, her despair.

ROSMER. About all this?

KROLL. No. The first time, it was because you were losing your faith, breaking with your own father's faith.

ROSMER (*forcefully*). You're wrong, Lars. It can't be.

KROLL. Why not?

ROSMER. Because all the time she was alive, I was debating, arguing with myself. And it was *my* fight, alone, no one knew. I don't think even Rebecca –

KROLL. Rebecca?

ROSMER. Well, Miss West. I call her Rebecca for . . . convenience.

KROLL. I've noticed.

ROSMER. It's impossible Beata knew anything about it. She'd have mentioned it. And she didn't. Not a single word.

KROLL. She was on her knees, poor creature, begging me to say something.

ROSMER. Then why didn't you?

KROLL. Don't you understand: at the time I thought she was ill. Mentally ill. Saying things like that about you – you! She came again, about a month later. She was calmer. Then, as she was going, she said, 'The White Horse will be there soon, at Rosmersholm.'

ROSMER. The White Horse. She talked about it, often.

KROLL. I tried to distract her. Such unhappiness. But she said, 'I haven't long. Johannes must hurry and marry Rebecca'.

ROSMER (*all but speechless*). What? Rebecca – ?

KROLL. That was Thursday afternoon. On Saturday afternoon she jumped into the millrace.

ROSMER. You could have warned us!

KROLL. You know she was always saying it was time for her to die.

ROSMER. All the same, you *should* have warned us.

KROLL. I meant to. But then it was too late.

ROSMER. And afterwards . . . why didn't you say anything? All this long time?

KROLL. What was the point? You'd enough to bear. I thought she was raving – till yesterday evening.

ROSMER. Now you don't think so?

KROLL. She was right, wasn't she? You *had* lost your faith?

ROSMER. How could she know? It's incomprehensible.

KROLL. Incomprehensible or not, she knew. And Johannes, the second thing – the second accusation.

ROSMER. What do you mean, accusation?

KROLL. I told you. She said she hadn't long, because –

ROSMER. I had to marry Rebecca.

KROLL. To quote her exact words: 'I haven't long. Johannes must hurry and marry Rebecca.'

ROSMER *stares at him a moment, then gets up.*

ROSMER. Lars, I know what you're saying.

KROLL. Oh, you do. And what do you answer?

ROSMER (*evenly, controlling himself*). To a charge like that? The only suitable answer would be to show you the door.

KROLL (*getting up*). Well. Fine.

ROSMER. Listen to me. For over a year now, to be exact, since Beata died, Rebecca West and I have lived here alone at Rosmersholm. All that time you've known what Beata accused us of. But I've never noticed you disapproving in the slightest of the fact that Rebecca and I were sharing this house.

KROLL. Till yesterday evening, when I discovered it was an atheist and a freethinker who were doing this sharing.

ROSMER. Oh! So atheists and freethinkers can't be pure, can't be moral, naturally moral –

KROLL. Without religion, there's no morality. I'm sure of that.

ROSMER. You think this applies to Rebecca and me? To our relationship?

KROLL. Why should you be different? I can't make exceptions. I can see no difference between freethinking and – hum.

ROSMER. Well, what?

KROLL. Free love, if you force me to say it.

ROSMER (*quietly*). Aren't you embarrassed? Saying this to me? Your oldest friend.

KROLL. That's *why* I'm saying it. I know how easily people influence you. Anyone. This Rebecca, I'm sorry, this Miss West, we know nothing about her. I tell you, Johannes, I won't let you go. Try, try to save yourself.

ROSMER. Save myself from what?

MRS HELSETH *opens the door and looks in.*

What is it?

MRS HELSETH. I was looking for Miss West.

ROSMER. She's not here.

MRS HELSETH. Isn't she?

She looks round the room.

That's funny.

Exit.

ROSMER. Well?

KROLL. Listen. What went on in secret while Beata was alive – and what's probably still going on – doesn't concern me. Your marriage was unhappy, I suppose that's some kind of excuse . . .

ROSMER. How little you know me.

KROLL. Don't interrupt. What I mean is: if this business with Miss West is to continue, you *must* keep quiet about the backsliding, the unfortunate lapse she's led you into. Let me finish. Let me finish. If you have to, believe and think what the Devil you like about anything you like. But keep your ideas to yourself. These are private matters. No need to shout them from the housetops.

ROSMER. I must. The position I'm in –

KROLL. You owe it to who you are, Johannes! For generations, Rosmersholm has been a beacon of decency and order, respect for what everyone who is anyone believes in. The whole area looks up to you. What would happen, what havoc would it cause, if people discovered you'd abandoned everything Rosmersholm has stood for?

ROSMER. Lars, I'm sorry. For generations the Rosmer family has brought nothing but darkness and oppression. I think it's my duty to bring light and cheerfulness.

KROLL. A fine ambition for the last of his line! Leave it alone. You're not good at it. You were born to be a scholar, in an ivory tower . . .

ROSMER. Perhaps. My part may be humble, but I insist on playing it, in the battle of life.

KROLL. Oh, the battle of life. You know what that'll be for you? A battle with your friends, a battle to the death.

ROSMER (*quietly*). They can't be all fanatics.

KROLL. You're innocent, Johannes. A trusting soul. You've no idea what storms are going to break.

MRS HELSETH *puts her head in again.*

MRS HELSETH. Miss West wants to know –

ROSMER. What?

MRS HELSETH. There's someone downstairs to see you.

ROSMER. The man who came yesterday?

MRS HELSETH. No. That Mortensgård.

ROSMER. Mortensgård!

KROLL. So soon. Things have gone this far so soon.

ROSMER. What does he want? Why didn't you send him packing?

MRS HELSETH. Miss West told me to ask you to see him.

ROSMER. Tell him I'm busy.

KROLL (*to* MRS HELSETH). No, Mrs Helseth. Send him up.

She goes. He takes his hat.

I'm retreating, for now. But the battle's by no means over.

ROSMER. Lars, I swear to you, I'm not involved with Mortensgård.

KROLL. I don't believe you. Not a word you say. I'll never believe you again. From now on, it's war between us. Never fear, we'll disarm you.

ROSMER. Lars, how can you do this?

KROLL. You ask me that? What about Beata?

ROSMER. Not that again.

KROLL. All right. You solve the millrace problem, let your conscience solve it. If you still have a conscience.

Enter PEDER MORTENSGÅRD, *quietly. He is a short, weedy man with sparse red hair and beard.* KROLL *gives him a look of hate.*

Well, well, the 'Searchlight' now. Blazing out from Rosmersholm.

He buttons his coat.

I can see my way *now*, no question.

MORTENSGÅRD (*mildly*). Whenever you need guidance, the Searchlight will be waiting.

KROLL. How kind you are. As always. Have you forgotten the commandment, 'Thou shalt not bear false witness against thy neighbour'?

MORTENSGÅRD. No need to teach me the commandments, Headmaster.

KROLL. Not even the sixth?

MORTENSGÅRD. If I needed instruction, I'm sure Mr Rosmer would oblige.

KROLL. Mr Rosmer! Mr Pastor Rosmer! Oh, he's just the man you need. I wish you joy of each other. Joy!

He goes out and slams the door. ROSMER *gazes after him, saying quietly to himself:*

ROSMER. No choice. (*To* MORTENSGÅRD.) Please tell me what you want, Mr Mortensgård.

MORTENSGÅRD. I came to say thank you to Miss West, for the kind note she sent yesterday.

ROSMER. I know about the note. Have you seen her?

MORTENSGÅRD. Yes, briefly. (*With a slight smile.*) I gather ideas have been changing here at Rosmersholm.

ROSMER. My views have changed. Considerably. No, entirely.

MORTENSGÅRD. Miss West was saying. That's why she wanted me to talk to you.

ROSMER. About what, Mr Mortensgård?

MORTENSGÅRD. Would you mind if I announced in the 'Searchlight' that you've come over to the cause of freedom and progress?

ROSMER. I'd be glad if you would.

MORTENSGÅRD. It'll be in tomorrow's paper. It'll cause a sensation. Pastor Rosmer of Rosmersholm working for the forces of light in this way too.

ROSMER. I don't understand.

MORTENSGÅRD. Nothing helps the moral standing of the Party more than winning over a convinced and serious Christian.

ROSMER (*somewhat astonished*). You mean Miss West didn't tell you . . . ?

MORTENSGÅRD. Tell me what? She was in a hurry. Said I should ask you myself.

ROSMER. I've left the Church. Freedom of thought, in everything. I've rejected Christian teaching. From now on, it's of no importance.

MORTENSGÅRD. I'm amazed. If the Moon fell out of the sky, I wouldn't be more . . . You say you reject . . .

ROSMER. I stand where you've been standing for years. You can announce that in the 'Searchlight' too.

MORTENSGÅRD. Ah, no. My dear Rosmer . . . excuse me . . . this wouldn't be the moment.

ROSMER. Not the moment?

MORTENSGÅRD. Later would be better.

ROSMER. I don't understand.

MORTENSGÅRD. Mr Rosmer, there are ways of doing these things. In my experience . . . The thing is, now that you've joined our movement – and Miss West says you want to take an active part – I imagine you'd like to make yourself as effective as possible.

ROSMER. Naturally.

MORTENSGÅRD. Thank you. The point is, Pastor, if you announce right away that you've left the Church, you tie your hands before you start.

ROSMER. You think so?

MORTENSGÅRD. Believe me, you'd not help the cause at all. We've all the freethinkers we need, we're falling over them. What we need is a Christian standpoint, one people respect. We need that badly. So your views on this matter are nobody else's business, and you should keep them to yourself. If you don't mind my saying so.

ROSMER. If I say I've left the Church, you won't accept me?

MORTENSGÅRD. Pastor Rosmer, I'm afraid I can't. For some time I've made it a rule not to support anyone or anything who denies the Church.

ROSMER. You've returned to the fold?

MORTENSGÅRD. That's irrelevant.

ROSMER. I see.

MORTENSGÅRD. I'm not a free agent. As you ought to remember.

ROSMER. Why not free?

MORTENSGÅRD. Because I'm a marked man.

ROSMER. Ah.

MORTENSGÅRD. Branded. I said you ought to remember. You branded me.

ROSMER. If I'd stood then where I stand today, I'd have been more forgiving.

MORTENSGÅRD. But it's too late now. You branded me for life. I imagine you've no idea what that feels like. But you will, Pastor Rosmer, any moment now.

ROSMER. *I* will?

MORTENSGÅRD. D'you think Kroll and his merry men will hold thir tongues about your 'departure'? I gather the 'County Telegraph' is frothing at the mouth already. You're a marked man, Mr Rosmer.

ROSMER. What can they do, Mr Mortensgård? I'm
  invulnerable. My personal life is blameless.

MORTENSGÅRD (*with a wintry smile*). A large claim, your
  Reverence.

ROSMER. Maybe. But true.

MORTENSGÅRD. Even if you ransacked your entire
  existence, the way you ransacked mine?

ROSMER. What are you talking about, exactly?

MORTENSGÅRD. One thing, exactly. Just one – but if your
  enemies get their teeth into it . . .

ROSMER. I insist you tell me.

MORTENSGÅRD. Pastor Rosmer, it's obvious.

ROSMER. Not to me.

MORTENSGÅRD. I'll spell it out, then. The letter. I have a
  letter, a very odd letter, written here in Rosmersholm.

ROSMER. The one from Miss West. What about it?

MORTENSGÅRD. Not that one. Another one. In my
  possession.

ROSMER. Another from Miss West?

MORTENSGÅRD. She didn't write it.

ROSMER. Who did, then?

MORTENSGÅRD. The late Mrs Rosmer.

ROSMER. Beata! Beata wrote *you* a letter?

MORTENSGÅRD. Exactly.

ROSMER. When?

MORTENSGÅRD. A few weeks before she died. Eighteen months ago. A very odd letter.

ROSMER. You know that at that time Mrs Rosmer was . . . deluded?

MORTENSGÅRD. I know a lot of people thought so. But that wasn't what made the letter odd. Something else entirely.

ROSMER. What on earth did my poor wife have to say to *you*?

MORTENSGÅRD. I have the letter at home. It starts with . . . something about the constant dread and terror she lives in . . . bad people all around . . . plotting to damage *you*, hurt *you* . . .

ROSMER. Me?

MORTENSGÅRD. It gets even odder.

ROSMER. Tell me. All of it.

MORTENSGÅRD. The late Mrs Rosmer begs me on her knees to be generous. She knows, she says, it was you who had me sacked from my teaching job, and implores me not to take revenge.

ROSMER. What on Earth was she afraid you'd do?

MORTENSGÅRD. She said, if I ever heard gossip of bad goings-on at Rosmersholm, I was to pay no attention. Bad people, she said, all they wanted was to make you sad.

ROSMER. That's in the letter?

MORTENSGÅRD. Mr Rosmer, I'll show you.

ROSMER. I still don't understand. What gossip?

MORTENSGÅRD. First, that you'd lost your faith. Mrs Rosmer denied it – then. Second, well . . .

ROSMER. What?

MORTENSGÅRD. The writing was more confused. Nothing sinful going on at Rosmersholm, she'd never been betrayed in any way, if I ever heard that kind of gossip, please would I keep it out of the 'Searchlight' . . .

ROSMER. Does she give any names?

MORTENSGÅRD. No.

ROSMER. Who brought you the letter?

MORTENSGÅRD. It was delivered after dark one evening.

ROSMER. If you'd made enquiries at the time, you'd have found that my unfortunate wife wasn't responsible for her actions.

MORTENSGÅRD. Pastor Rosmer, I made enquiries. And that wasn't the way it seemed to me.

ROSMER. It wasn't? Never mind. This garbled letter – why do you bring it up now?

MORTENSGÅRD. To show you how careful you need to be.

ROSMER. In the way I live my life?

MORTENSGÅRD. Remember, from now on you're not 'invulnerable'.

ROSMER. You really think I'm hiding something.

MORTENSGÅRD. I think, when people set themselves free, they should be able to do anything they like. But I repeat, be careful. If anything gets out that upsets people's prejudices, the whole Movement suffers. Pastor Rosmer, I'll say good morning.

ROSMER. Good morning.

MORTENSGÅRD. I'll go straight to the office and put the good news in 'The Searchlight'.

ROSMER. Yes, all of it.

MORTENSGÅRD. As much as the public needs to know.

He bows and exits. ROSMER *stands watching him go downstairs, waiting till the sound of the front door closing. Then he calls softly.*

ROSMER. Rebecca! Re – hum. (*Louder.*) Mrs Helseth! Isn't Miss West down there?

MRS HELSETH (*from the hall*). No, sir. Not here.

The curtain at the back is drawn, and REBECCA *comes in from the bedroom.*

REBECCA. Johannes.

ROSMER (*turning*). You were in the bedroom. My dear, what were you doing?

REBECCA (*going to him*). Listening.

ROSMER. Oh, Rebecca!

REBECCA. How could he *talk* like that? My house-coat . . .

ROSMER. You mean, Kroll. You were –

REBECCA. I wanted to know what was lurking in his mind.

ROSMER. I'd have told you.

REBECCA. Not all of it. And not in his words.

ROSMER. You heard it all?

REBECCA. Most of it. I had to go down a moment when Mortensgård arrived.

ROSMER. But you came up again.

REBECCA. My dear, don't be angry.

ROSMER. It's for you to choose. You're a free agent. What d'you think of it all? I've never needed you so much as I do today.

REBECCA. We've been expecting this for a long time. Both of us.

ROSMER. Not *this*.

REBECCA. What d'you mean?

ROSMER. I knew our beautiful, innocent friendship was bound to be misinterpreted one day. Smeared. Not by Kroll, I never imagined *he'd* . . . The rest of them, with their vulgar minds and beady little eyes. Oh yes, I knew exactly why we kept it secret. A dangerous secret.

REBECCA. But why should we care what they think? *We* know we're innocent.

ROSMER. Do we? Do I? Till today, I did. But now, oh Rebecca –

REBECCA. What, now?

ROSMER. What Beata wrote. How can I explain – ?

REBECCA (*with force*). Forget Beata! Don't think about Beata! She's dead and buried. You were beginning to forget her.

ROSMER. After what I've heard, it's as if she'd come to life again.

REBECCA. Johannes, no. Don't say that.

ROSMER. We have to talk about this. Such a dreadful misunderstanding. What made her think it?

REBECCA. She was nearly out of her mind. Don't you think so now?

ROSMER. How can I be sure? And even if she was –

REBECCA. What, then?

ROSMER. We still have to ask what drove her to it, what pushed her?

REBECCA. What good does it do, brooding on it?

ROSMER. I can't help it.

REBECCA. You'll harm yourself, the same questions, day in day out.

ROSMER. I must have given it away. Without realising. She must have noticed. How happy I was. From the moment you arrived.

REBECCA. And supposing she did, Johannes?

ROSMER. She must have noticed. We read the same books. Discussed them. New ideas: we were drawn together. I don't understand. I was so careful, to protect her. When I think . . . I did everything I could to keep her away from all that we . . . Rebecca, didn't I?

REBECCA. Of course you did.

ROSMER. And so did you. Then, even so . . . It's appalling! She must have . . . the state she was in . . . never speaking . . . watching . . . noticing . . . misunderstanding . . .

REBECCA. I wish I'd never come.

ROSMER. To think what she must have suffered. In silence. All that bile, foul thoughts, her poor sick brain . . . Did she say anything to you, Rebecca, ever, give you any hint?

REBECCA. If she had, d'you think I'd still be here?

ROSMER. Of course not. To fight like that, desperate, alone
. . . and then to win a victory like that, a cry of agony, an
accusation, in the millrace . . .

REBECCA. Johannes, listen. If you could bring her back,
back here to Rosmersholm . . . if you had the power . . .
would you do it?

ROSMER. Who knows what I'd do or wouldn't do? All I can
think of, the one thing I think of . . . it's gone, forever.

REBECCA. You should start to live, Johannes. You *were*
starting. You set yourself free, from all of it. You were
happy, light-hearted –

ROSMER. And then this happened. It's destroying me.

REBECCA. D'you remember how it was? How we sat
downstairs in the dark, planning our futures, helping each
other? You wanted to snatch real life, the real life all round
you. Pass from family to family, like a welcome guest,
taking them freedom, winning hearts and minds, ennobling
people. Ennobling them.

ROSMER. Noble, and happy.

REBECCA. Happy.

ROSMER. If you're happy, you're ennobled.

REBECCA. Even if you're grieving.

ROSMER. If you put it behind you.

REBECCA. That's what you have to do.

ROSMER. I can't. I'll never be sure. There'll always be a
shadow, a question. I'll never lose myself in what makes
life worth living.

REBECCA. What's that, Johannes?

ROSMER. A pure conscience.

REBECCA. Ah.

Short pause.

ROSMER. It's incredible, the way she must have gathered her evidence, put it all together. First, she begins to doubt my faith. What put that in her mind? Never mind, she convinced herself. And after that, everything was possible. She could imagine what she liked.

He runs his hands through his hair.

My mind's on fire. I can't control it. Full of images. Crowding in on me. Never-ending. To remind me of the dead.

REBECCA. The White Horse of Rosmersholm.

ROSMER. Galloping, in silence, in darkness . . .

REBECCA. Images. You were snatching real life, and now you let go, because of images?

ROSMER. Rebecca, what else can I do? How can I escape from this?

REBECCA. By a new relationship.

ROSMER. What new relationship?

REBECCA. With the world. With life, work, action. Don't sit here brooding on images.

ROSMER. A new relationship.

He walks to the door, then comes back to her.

One thing, Rebecca. You must wonder too.

REBECCA. What, wonder?

ROSMER. After today, what *our* relationship will be.

REBECCA. Friends. We'll always be friends.

ROSMER. I mean, what brought us together. What unites us. Our faith that a man and a woman can have a pure and innocent relationship –

REBECCA. What about it?

ROSMER. I mean, for that to work, life has to be peaceful, contented, calm –

REBECCA. Go on.

ROSMER. But now, Rebecca! My life's to be one of struggle, conflict, violent emotion. Rebecca, I want it! I won't be silenced. No one will dictate my life, no one alive, or . . . not alive.

REBECCA. Be free, Johannes, free.

ROSMER. Don't you understand? The best way to free myself, shake free of them, these memories, the past, don't you understand?

REBECCA. What is it?

ROSMER. Instead of them, a new reality, a live reality –

REBECCA. Live . . . ? What d'you mean?

ROSMER. Rebecca, if I asked you . . . my second wife –

REBECCA *is silent for a moment, then shouts with joy.*

REBECCA. Marry you?

ROSMER. The two of us, one. The gap she left, completed.

REBECCA. I'm to take Beata's place?

ROSMER. She'll be gone forever.

REBECCA (*suddenly, trembling*). Do you really think so?

ROSMER. It must be! I can't – won't – go through life with a corpse on my back. Rebecca, help me. Let's blot out the past in freedom, in joy, in passion. You'll be the only wife I've ever had.

REBECCA (*controlling herself*). Don't ever talk of this again. I won't be your wife.

ROSMER. You mean you'll never love me? Our friendship isn't tinged with love already?

REBECCA. Johannes, don't say that!

ROSMER. I mean it. It's possible. What we have – oh Rebecca, don't you feel it . . . feel it?

REBECCA (*controlling herself*). If you go on with this, I'm leaving forever.

ROSMER. You can't. It's impossible.

REBECCA. I can't be your wife. That's what's impossible.

ROSMER (*bewildered*). Why not? Why d'you say you can't?

REBECCA. Dearest friend, don't ask, for your sake, my sake. Don't.

She goes towards the door left.

ROSMER. But how can I think of anything else?

REBECCA. You must. It's settled.

ROSMER. Between you and me?

REBECCA. Yes.

ROSMER. You'll never leave Rosmersholm.

REBECCA. If you ask me again, that's settled too.

ROSMER. How, settled?

REBECCA. I'll go where Beata went. Johannes, believe it.

ROSMER. Rebecca –

REBECCA. Believe it.

Exit.

ROSMER. What's happened?

End of Act Two.

ACT THREE

The sitting-room. The window and hall doors are open. Bright morning sun streams in. REBECCA, *dressed as in Act One, is watering and arranging flowers by the window. Her work is on the armchair.* MRS HELSETH *is dusting furniture with a feather duster.*

REBECCA (*after a moment*). Mr Rosmer's late this morning.

MRS HELSETH. Yes, Miss. He'll be down directly.

REBECCA. Have you seen him?

MRS HELSETH. When I took up his coffee. He went into his bedroom to finish dressing.

REBECCA. I asked because yesterday he seemed out of sorts.

MRS HELSETH. I wonder if something's wrong between him and his brother-in-law.

REBECCA. Doctor Kroll? What, d'you think?

MRS HELSETH. I'm sure I can't say. Unless that Mortensgård's been making trouble.

REBECCA. D'you know anything about him?

MRS HELSETH. I most certainly do not. How can you ask, Miss? A man like that!

REBECCA. You mean his newspaper?

MRS HELSETH. It's not just that. You must have heard, Miss: he had a child by a married lady. Her husband had left her.

REBECCA. I've heard. But that was long before I came here.

MRS HELSETH. It's true, he was young. And she should have known better. He wanted to marry her, but of course he couldn't. And I'm not saying he hasn't been punished. But Heavens, how things have changed for him! The whole world's after him.

REBECCA. Poor people taking him their problems.

MRS HELSETH. Not just poor people, either.

REBECCA. What d'you mean?

MRS HELSETH (*vigorously dusting the sofa*). The last people you might imagine, Miss.

REBECCA (*at the flowers*). You don't *know* that, Mrs Helseth. You're guessing.

MRS HELSETH. You think so, Miss? I know what I know. I'll tell you. Once I delivered him a letter, myself in person.

REBECCA (*turning to look at her*). Did you?

MRS HELSETH. One written here at Rosmersholm.

REBECCA. Really?

MRS HELSETH. Yes, Miss, I promise you. Best notepaper, sealing wax . . .

REBECCA. And you delivered it. Mrs Helseth, it's obvious who wrote it.

MRS HELSETH. Yes, Miss.

REBECCA. Something poor Mrs Rosmer, in the state she was in −

MRS HELSETH. Now *you* said that, Miss, not me.

REBECCA. But what was in the letter? I'm sorry, you can't possibly know.

MRS HELSETH. Hum, and what if I do?

REBECCA. She told you what she was writing?

MRS HELSETH. Not exactly. Mortensgård asked me questions, after he'd read it, up the hill, down the hill. I soon worked out what was in it.

REBECCA. And that was . . . ? Mrs Helseth, please. Tell me.

MRS HELSETH. I can't Miss. Not for all the world.

REBECCA. I thought we were friends.

MRS HELSETH. Lord save me from telling you *that*, Miss. Something dreadful they'd got the poor sick lady to imagine.

REBECCA. Who had?

MRS HELSETH. Bad people, Miss. Wicked people.

REBECCA. Wicked?

MRS HELSETH. Yes, Miss. Wicked.

REBECCA. Who d'you think they were?

MRS HELSETH. I know what I think. But Lord save me from saying. There's a lady in town, Miss . . . hum . . .

REBECCA. You mean Mrs Kroll.

MRS HELSETH. Lady high and mighty. Nose in the air with us. And no time for you, Miss, either.

REBECCA. When Mrs Rosmer wrote to Mortensgård, d'you think she was *herself*?

MRS HELSETH. Who can say, Miss? Another person's mind. I think she was sane enough.

REBECCA. But when she found she couldn't have children
. . . Didn't that . . . ? I mean, didn't it begin then?

MRS HELSETH. Poor soul. It was a dreadful blow.

REBECCA *takes up her crochet and sits by the window.*

REBECCA. Even so, for Mr Rosmer, it was perhaps for the
best.

MRS HELSETH. Pardon, Miss?

REBECCA. Not having children. Don't you think so?

MRS HELSETH. I don't know what to answer.

REBECCA. For the best, believe me. Pastor Rosmer and a
houseful of crying children . . .

MRS HELSETH. Children never cry at Rosmersholm, Miss.

REBECCA. Pardon?

MRS HELSETH. So long as anyone can remember, no child
has ever cried at Rosmersholm.

REBECCA. How peculiar.

MRS HELSETH. It runs in the family. And there's
something even stranger. When they grow up, they never
laugh. Never, as long as they live.

REBECCA. You're making this up.

MRS HELSETH. Miss: have you ever seen Mr Rosmer
laughing?

REBECCA. Now you mention it, I don't think so. But in this
part of the country, I've never seen *anyone* laughing.

MRS HELSETH. They never do, Miss. It started here at
Rosmersholm, and spread everywhere. It was like an
infection.

REBECCA. Mrs Helseth, you're a very clever woman.

MRS HELSETH. Now don't you sit there making fun of me, Miss.

She listens.

Sh! He's coming. He doesn't like dusters.

Exit right. Enter ROSMER *from the hall. He has his hat and stick.*

ROSMER. Good morning, Rebecca.

REBECCA. Johannes, good morning. (*Pause, as she goes on working.*) Going out?

ROSMER. That's right.

REBECCA. It's a beautiful day.

ROSMER. You didn't look in this morning.

REBECCA. Not today.

ROSMER. You will, again?

REBECCA. I don't know yet, Johannes.

ROSMER. Has the post arrived?

REBECCA. The 'County Telegraph', that's all.

ROSMER. The Telegraph!

REBECCA. It's on the table. ·

ROSMER (*putting down his hat and stick*). Is there anything – ?

REBECCA. Yes.

ROSMER. Why didn't you send it up?

REBECCA. You'll read it soon enough.

ROSMER. Well, then.

He stands by the table and starts reading the paper.

What? ' . . . warn our readers to beware of deserters . . . '
Rebecca, that's me they mean. A deserter!

REBECCA. They don't name names.

ROSMER. It's obvious. (*reading*) ' . . . secret traitors . . . ',
' . . . Judases, who time their betrayal for maximum
personal advantage . . . ', ' . . . trample their distinguished
ancestors . . . ', ' . . . hoping for rewards from those who
are temporarily our masters . . . '. (*Putting the paper down.*)
They write this: people who've known me for years, been
friends for years. They don't believe it, but they write it.
Every word is a lie, they know that and still they write it.

REBECCA. There's more.

ROSMER (*picking up the paper again*). ' . . . inexperience,
naivety mere excuses . . . ', ' . . . pernicious influence,
extending to matters which for the moment we don't want
to report or condemn . . . '. (*Looking at her.*) What matters?

REBECCA. Well, obviously: me.

ROSMER (*putting down the paper*). They'll do *anything*.

REBECCA. After all they say about Mortensgård.

ROSMER. It's got to stop. It's grotesque, it tramples human
decency. I have to stop it, to open it up, bring light. And
I'll be glad to do it.

REBECCA. Yes, Johannes. You're the man for this.

ROSMER. If I could rouse them, make them angry with
themselves, ashamed, persuade them to live in peace and
friendship . . . oh, Rebecca!

REBECCA. *That's* the fight you have to win.

ROSMER. Win happiness, freedom. No more envy or competition. Every eye fixed on the same goal, every mind, every soul pressing onwards, upwards, the goal they were born for! Happiness for all, through all!

He happens to glance out of the window, starts and says bleakly:

Ah. But not through me.

REBECCA. What d'you mean?

ROSMER. Not for me, either.

REBECCA. Johannes, what's the matter?

ROSMER. To be happy, Rebecca, dear Rebecca, you have to feel calm, guiltfree . . .

REBECCA. Guiltfree.

ROSMER. You have no guilt. But I –

REBECCA. What guilt do you have?

ROSMER (*pointing out of the window*). The millrace.

REBECCA. Oh, Johannes . . .

MRS HELSETH *comes to the door.*

MRS HELSETH. Miss West . . .

REBECCA. Not now. In a moment.

MRS HELSETH. Just a word, Miss.

REBECCA *goes to her.* She and MRS HELSETH *murmur a moment together, then* MRS HELSETH *nods and exits.*

ROSMER (*uneasily*). Anything for me?

REBECCA. Domestic matters. Johannes, you need fresh air. Go out for a good long walk.

ROSMER (*picking up his hat*). We'll both go.

REBECCA. My dear, I can't just now. You go. And shake off these gloomy thoughts. Promise me.

ROSMER. I never will. I don't think I can.

REBECCA. There's nothing in them. Don't let them affect you.

ROSMER. What if there is something in them? I was thinking about it all night. What if Beata was right after all?

REBECCA. What d'you mean?

ROSMER. When she imagined I loved you.

REBECCA. That.

ROSMER (*putting his hat on the table*). I can't get it out of my mind. Were we deceiving ourselves all the time? When we thought it was friendship . . .

REBECCA. And all the time it was –

ROSMER. Love, Rebecca. Even when Beata was alive, it was you I thought about, longed for. With you I felt peace, contentment, fulfilment. Like children, Rebecca, the way children are friends – pure, without dreams, without longings. Tell me!

REBECCA. I don't know what to answer.

ROSMER. We were intertwined – with each other, for each other – and we took it for friendship. It wasn't, Rebecca. From the moment we met, a marriage of the soul – that's why I feel guilty. I'd no right to such happiness, at Beata's expense.

REBECCA. No right to be happy?

ROSMER. She saw what we had, with the eyes of love she saw it, judged it. What else could she do? What else could she think?

REBECCA. *She* thought! *She* thought! How can you blame yourself?

ROSMER. Her love for me, the love it was: she *had* to drown herself. My dear, it can't be wished away. I'll never get over it.

REBECCA. But the cause, the beautiful cause. Fix your thoughts on that!

ROSMER. It won't be achieved. At least, not by me. Not after what I know now.

REBECCA. Why not by you?

ROSMER. Because no cause can triumph if it starts in sin.

REBECCA (*with force*). For Heaven's sake! Inherited ideas, inherited doubts, inherited scruples. The dead, rushing back to Rosmersholm like galloping white horses. That's what people say, and I think it's true.

ROSMER. I can't shake it off: that's what matters. I tell you, Rebecca, for a cause to succeed its champion must be entirely happy and entirely guiltfree.

REBECCA. Johannes, you *must* be happy?

ROSMER. Yes, Rebecca.

REBECCA. A man who never laughs?

ROSMER. I *can* be happy. Believe me.

REBECCA. Go for your walk. A good, long walk. Here's your hat. Your stick.

ROSMER. You're sure you won't come?

REBECCA. I can't just now.

ROSMER. All right. You be with me in spirit.

Exit through the hall. REBECCA *watches until he's gone, then goes and opens the door right.*

REBECCA. All right, Mrs Helseth. He can come in now.

Enter KROLL *right. He bows formally, silently. He keeps hold of his hat.*

KROLL. Gone out?

REBECCA. Yes.

KROLL. Is it long, usually?

REBECCA. Usually. But he's unpredictable today. So if you don't want to meet him –

KROLL. It's you I want to speak to. In private.

REBECCA. Then you'd better sit down, Doctor Kroll.

She sits by the window. He takes a chair, and sits near her.

KROLL. Miss West, you've no idea how distressed this makes me, to the bottom of my heart: this change that's come over him.

REBECCA. We expected as much, to start with.

KROLL. To start with?

REBECCA. Johannes was convinced you'd join him.

KROLL. *I* would?

REBECCA. And all his other friends.

KROLL. You see! That proves it. He has no judgement, about other people, about reality.

REBECCA. Well. Now he feels he has to set himself free, in every way –

KROLL. I'm sure he doesn't.

REBECCA. I – pardon?

KROLL. I think all this comes from *you*.

REBECCA. Who put that in your head, Doctor Kroll – your wife?

KROLL. Never mind. The point is, I believe it. And the more I think about your behaviour, ever since you first arrived here . . .

REBECCA (*gazing at him*). I seem to remember a time, dear Doctor, when you felt quite differently about me. Quite differently.

KROLL (*in a low voice*). You could bewitch anyone you wanted.

REBECCA. And you think I wanted – ?

KROLL. It's obvious. I'm not a fool. You wanted a position at Rosmersholm, a chance to take root here . . . and I was useful to you. It's obvious.

REBECCA. You seem to forget it was Beata who begged and implored me to come here.

KROLL. Oh, you bewitched her too. What d'you call what she felt for you? Friendship? It was adoration, she idolised you, it was . . . a love affair. Nothing else but that.

REBECCA. Please remember your sister's state of mind. I don't think anyone could accuse me of . . . hysteria.

KROLL. Oh no. That's why you're so dangerous. You plan everything in advance, work out exactly what will happen. Your heart is ice.

REBECCA. You think so?

KROLL. I'm certain. How else could you have stayed here, year after year, without faltering for a moment? You knew just what you wanted, and now you've got it. He's in your power, entirely in your power. And to do that, all you had to do was make him miserable.

REBECCA. That's not true. *You* made him miserable.

KROLL. *I* did?

REBECCA. You made him think he caused what happened to Beata.

KROLL. That makes him miserable?

REBECCA. What d'you think? A man so sensitive –

KROLL (*sarcastically*). A free mind, a free spirit – I'd have thought he could cope with thoughts like that. And that's the point. I knew what would happen. *Their* blood runs in his veins, the people round these walls, generation after generation – how could he cut himself free of *them*?

REBECCA. A Rosmer of Rosmersholm. You're right.

KROLL. If you'd felt anything at all for him, you'd have remembered that. But of course you didn't. How could you? Between where you came from, and he came from, the gulf is unbridgeable!

REBECCA. What on earth do you mean?

KROLL. I'm talking about background, Miss West.

REBECCA. I admit my family are working-class –

KROLL. I don't mean family background. Moral background.

REBECCA. I don't understand.

KROLL. The background of your birth.

REBECCA. What d'you mean?

KROLL. I think it explains everything about you.

REBECCA. Please say what you mean.

KROLL. Oh, you understand. Otherwise, why did you let Doctor West adopt you?

REBECCA (*getting up*). *That's* what you mean.

KROLL. Why did you take his name? Your mother's name was Gamvik.

REBECCA (*walking across the room*). Doctor Kroll, my *father's* name was Gamvik.

KROLL. Your mother's . . . occupation must have meant she was often in contact with the Doctor.

REBECCA. Naturally.

KROLL. And then, as soon as she dies, he takes you in. He ill-treats you, and still you stay. You know he won't leave you a penny – all you ever got was a box of books – and still you stay, you put up with him, you nurse him.

REBECCA (*with scorn*). And your explanation for all this is that there was something immoral, criminal, about my birth?

KROLL. I think the reason you cared for him was instinct, filial instinct. I think your origin explains your entire behaviour.

REBECCA. The whole thing's nonsense! And I can prove it. Doctor West didn't come to Finmark until after I was born.

KROLL. I'm sorry, Miss West. He settled there one year before. I've checked.

REBECCA. You're completely mistaken.

KROLL. The other day you told me you were twenty-nine. In your thirtieth year.

REBECCA. Did I?

KROLL. And I calculate from that –

REBECCA. Don't bother. I'll tell you: I'm a year older than I say I am.

KROLL (*with an unbelieving smile*). Now, really? Why on earth is that?

REBECCA. When I reached twenty-five, I thought I was getting too old still not to be married. So I lied about my age.

KROLL. An emancipated woman! You've *views* about the right age for marriage?

REBECCA. It's ridiculous. But some things stick. We can't shake them off.

KROLL. Well, it doesn't affect my calculations. Doctor West visited Finmark, briefly, the year before he was appointed there.

REBECCA (*quickly*). That's not true.

KROLL. It isn't?

REBECCA. My mother would have said.

KROLL. And she didn't.

REBECCA. *He* didn't either. Doctor West.

KROLL. Perhaps they had good reasons for losing a year. *You* did, Miss West. Perhaps it's a family tradition.

REBECCA. It's nonsense. You're trying to trick me. It's impossible.

KROLL. My dear Miss West, what on earth's the matter? I'm amazed. What on Earth am I to think?

REBECCA. Nothing. You're to think nothing.

KROLL. In that case, you really must explain. Why on earth are you so upset?

REBECCA (*controlling herself*). It's perfectly simple, Doctor Kroll. D'you think I *want* people here to think I'm illegitimate?

KROLL. Hum. Well, let's accept that explanation – for now. You realise it means you have yet another prejudice?

REBECCA. I realise.

KROLL. It seems to me, this is what it's like, your free-thinking. You read a few ideas, revolutionary opinions, snippets of information on this or that discovery, all of them turning upside-down what everyone's always believed and stood for. But it's all in the mind, Miss West. On the surface. Doesn't penetrate the blood.

REBECCA. Perhaps you're right.

KROLL. Oh yes. Think about it. And if that's the case with you, what about Johannes? It's madness, hurtling to disaster, for him to think of admitting he's left the Church. You said yourself, he's sensitive. Imagine: he'll be disowned, driven out of the circle he's always belonged to, attacked by everyone who matters. He can't survive. He won't.

REBECCA. He can't draw back now.

KROLL. Of course he can. What's happened can be hushed up, or at least explained: a lapse, regrettable, deplorable, but temporary. It can be done – but only one condition.

REBECCA. Namely?

KROLL. Miss West, you must make him legalise the relationship.

REBECCA. With me, you mean?

KROLL. Exactly.

REBECCA. You're convinced that our relationship needs to be . . . legalised?

KROLL. I prefer not to enquire too closely. I do know that of all the prejudices hardest to break down, the worst is –

REBECCA. About male-female relationships?

KROLL. To put it bluntly.

REBECCA *goes to the window and looks out.*

REBECCA. I think . . . Doctor Kroll, I nearly said, I wish you were right.

KROLL. What's the matter?

REBECCA. Let's change the subject. Look, he's coming.

KROLL. So soon. I'd better go.

REBECCA (*going to him*). Please stay. There's something I want you to hear.

KROLL. I don't want to see him.

REBECCA. If you don't, you'll regret it later. I'll never ask you for anything else.

KROLL *looks at her in surprise, puts down his hat.*

KROLL. Whatever you say, Miss West.

Pause. Then ROSMER *enters from the hall. He sees* KROLL, *and stops in the doorway.*

ROSMER. You, here.

REBECCA. He didn't want to, darling.

KROLL (*involuntarily*). Darling!

REBECCA. We call each other darling, Doctor Kroll. Because of our . . . relationship.

KROLL. That's what you wanted me to hear?

REBECCA. And something else.

ROSMER (*coming forward*). What's the purpose of this visit?

KROLL. I wanted to try once more, to stop you, win you back . . .

ROSMER (*pointing to the paper*). After *that*?

KROLL. I didn't write that.

ROSMER. Did you make any effort at all to prevent it?

KROLL. I fight for a cause, remember. And it wasn't my decision.

REBECCA *rips the paper to pieces and stuffs them in the stove.*

REBECCA. There. It's gone. Forget about it. It'll never happen again, Johannes.

KROLL. Well, I think that's really up to you.

REBECCA. Sit down, darling. All three of us, sit down. I'll tell you everything.

ROSMER. Rebecca, what's the matter? I've not seen you like this. What is it?

REBECCA. I've decided. (*Sitting.*) Doctor Kroll, you too.

KROLL *sits on the sofa.*

ROSMER. What have you decided?

REBECCA. To give you back what you need to live your life. Johannes, set free your conscience.

ROSMER. What do you mean?

REBECCA. All I have to do is tell you something.

ROSMER. Tell me something . . .

REBECCA. When I came south from Finmark, with Doctor West, it seemed as though a new, vast world was opening up for me. Doctor West had taught me as much as he could, all kinds of things, all I knew till then. (*Struggling with herself.*) And then . . .

KROLL. What then?

ROSMER. Rebecca, I know all this.

REBECCA (*controlling herself*). All you need to know.

KROLL. I think I should leave.

REBECCA. No. Doctor Kroll, please stay. (*To* ROSMER.) That's how it was. I wanted to share in the new age that was dawning, the new ideas. One day, Doctor Kroll told me how Ulrik Brendel had had such an influence on you when you were a boy. I thought . . . I might be able to carry on his work.

ROSMER. You had a *plan* when you came here?

REBECCA. We'd march to freedom together, I thought. Side by side, further and further forward. But you couldn't. Between you and freedom there was that barrier, grim, unconquerable –

ROSMER. What barrier?

REBECCA. Johannes, you'd grow into freedom only in fresh, bright sunshine. And you were pining, sickening, choked in that marriage.

ROSMER. You've never talked like this before.

REBECCA. I didn't want to scare you away.

KROLL (*nodding at* ROSMER). You hear what she says?

REBECCA (*continuing*). But it was obvious what had to be done if you were to be free. So I went to work.

ROSMER. What are you talking about?

KROLL. *You* – ?

REBECCA. Johannes . . .

She gets up.

Sit still. You too, Doctor Kroll. It has to be said. It wasn't you, Johannes. You had nothing to do with it. *I* did it, *I* made Beata believe . . .

ROSMER (*jumping up*). Rebecca!

KROLL (*getting up*). You made her –

REBECCA. The path to the millrace. That's all. Now you both know.

ROSMER (*as if stunned*). I don't understand. What does she mean? I don't –

KROLL. Maybe you don't, but I do.

ROSMER. But what can you possibly have told her? There was nothing, absolutely nothing.

REBECCA. She . . . was informed that you were shaking yourself free of the old beliefs.

ROSMER. But I wasn't, then.

REBECCA. I knew you would be.

KROLL (*nodding to* ROSMER). You see.

ROSMER. What else? Tell me!

REBECCA. I begged her, on my knees, to let me go away
from Rosmersholm.

ROSMER. Why then?

REBECCA. Oh, I wanted to stay. But I told her it would be
best for all of us, that I ought to go. I made it clear that if
I stayed I couldn't – wouldn't – answer for what
happened.

ROSMER. You did this, said this . . .

REBECCA. Yes, Johannes.

ROSMER. This is what you meant? 'I went to work.'

REBECCA. It's what I meant.

Pause.

ROSMER. Rebecca, is there more to confess?

REBECCA. No.

KROLL. I think there is.

REBECCA (*looking at him*). What more could there be?

KROLL. Didn't you end by making Beata think it was
essential that you went away? Not 'best', essential. For
your own sake, for Johannes' sake, that you left
Rosmersholm as soon as possible? Didn't you?

REBECCA (*low*). I may have suggested it.

ROSMER. And all this – she believed it. My poor, sick wife believed it. A tissue of lies, and she believed it. (*Looking up at* REBECCA.) She didn't say a word of it to me. Not a word. Rebecca, I see in your face, you persuaded her not to.

REBECCA. She had it in her head that because she couldn't have children, she had no right to be here. She felt that she owed it to you, to blot herself out.

ROSMER. You didn't try to stop her?

REBECCA. No.

KROLL. You encouraged her. Didn't you? Answer me!

REBECCA. She may have thought so.

ROSMER. She was completely under your control. And she did blot herself out! How could you do it? Play games like this – how could you?

REBECCA. Two lives were at stake, Johannes. I had to choose.

KROLL. What right had *you* to choose?

REBECCA (*with force*). D'you imagine I was icy then? Cold, calculating . . . ? As I stand here now, telling you now? I was different then! We have two kinds of will in us, we humans. I wanted Beata away, I didn't care how, but I never imagined she *would* go. I was inching forward, one step at a time. And at every step, a voice said, 'Stop! No further!' – and I couldn't. I had to go on. One little step more. Another, another . . . and then it happened. That's how things *are*.

Pause.

ROSMER. What'll happen now? To you?

REBECCA. It doesn't matter.

KROLL. Don't you feel *remorse*?

REBECCA (*coldly*). I'm sorry, Doctor Kroll: *my* business. *I'll* deal with it.

KROLL (*to* ROSMER). This is the woman you were living with! (*Looking round at the pictures.*) If the dead could see us now!

ROSMER. Are you going back to town?

KROLL (*taking his hat*). The sooner the better.

ROSMER (*taking his hat*). I'll come with you.

KROLL. I *thought* we hadn't lost you!

ROSMER. Lars, come on.

Exeunt by the hall, without a glance at REBECCA. *Pause. Then she goes to the window and looks at the flowers. She speaks to herself, almost under her breath.*

REBECCA. Still not the footbridge. He still goes round. Never across the millrace. Well.

She goes and pulls the bell. After a moment, enter MRS HELSETH, *right.*

MRS HELSETH. Yes, Miss?

REBECCA. Mrs Helseth, please fetch my cases down from the attic.

MRS HELSETH. Your cases, Miss?

REBECCA. The brown one. The sealskin one.

MRS HELSETH. Yes, Miss. But Heavens above, you're not going somewhere, Miss?

REBECCA. Yes, Mrs Helseth.

MRS HELSETH. Now? Today?

REBECCA. As soon as I've packed.

MRS HELSETH. But you are coming back?

REBECCA. Never.

MRS HELSETH. Dear lord, what will it be like without you? Just when the Pastor was beginning to be so happy and comfortable.

REBECCA. Mrs Helseth, today something scared me.

MRS HELSETH. What, Miss?

REBECCA. I thought I saw white horses.

MRS HELSETH. In daylight!

REBECCA. They come whenever they like, the White Horses of Rosmersholm. (*Changed tone.*) The cases, Mrs Helseth.

MRS HELSETH. Yes, Miss. The trunk.

Exeunt right.

End of Act Three.

ACT FOUR

The sitting-room. Late evening. A shaded lamp is lit on the table.
REBECCA *is standing at the table, putting small things into a*
travelling bag. Her cloak, hat and the white shawl she has been
crocheting are over the back of the sofa.

Enter MRS HELSETH, *right. She seems subdued and ill at ease.*

MRS HELSETH. The cases are down, Miss. All of them, in
the kitchen passage.

REBECCA. Thank you. You've ordered the carriage?

MRS HELSETH. The coachman wants to know what time.

REBECCA. Eleven, I think. The boat goes at midnight.

MRS HELSETH (*hesitantly*). But Mr Rosmer? If he isn't home
by then?

REBECCA. I'll go all the same. If I don't see him, tell him
I'll write. A long letter. Tell him.

MRS HELSETH. Yes, writing. No harm in writing. But Miss,
I think you ought to try and talk to him again.

REBECCA. Perhaps. Perhaps not.

MRS HELSETH. That I should see today! Who'd have
imagined – ?

REBECCA. What *did* you imagine, Mrs Helseth?

MRS HELSETH. To tell you the truth, Miss, I thought the
Pastor would be more honest.

REBECCA. More *honest?*

MRS HELSETH. Yes.

REBECCA. What on earth do you mean?

MRS HELSETH. It's only right, Miss. He shouldn't wriggle out of it like this.

REBECCA. Mrs Helseth, why *do* you think I'm leaving?

MRS HELSETH. Because you have to, Miss. I mean . . . But even so, Mr Rosmer's behaving very badly. At least Mortensgård had an excuse: the woman's husband was still alive. *They* couldn't marry, however much they wanted. But Mr Rosmer . . . well . . .

REBECCA. D'you really think and I and Mr Rosmer – ?

MRS HELSETH. No, never. Not till today, at least.

REBECCA. Why today?

MRS HELSETH. Those things in the paper, awful things about Mr Rosmer –

REBECCA. Oh.

MRS HELSETH. I mean, if a man goes over to Mortensgård's religion . . . he's capable of anything. That's what I say.

REBECCA. But what about me, Mrs Helseth? What d'you think of me?

MRS HELSETH. Bless you, Miss, it's not your fault. A woman on her own, it's easy to be caught offguard. We *are* all human, Miss.

REBECCA. Exactly. We are all human. D'you hear something?

MRS HELSETH. Dear God, I think he's coming.

REBECCA. No choice, then. So be it.

Enter ROSMER *from the hall. He glances at the packing, then at* REBECCA.

ROSMER. What does this mean?

REBECCA. I'm leaving.

ROSMER. Right away?

REBECCA. Yes. (*To* MRS HELSETH.) Eleven o'clock, then.

MRS HELSETH. Yes, Miss.

Exit right. Pause.

ROSMER. Where are you going?

REBECCA. I'm taking the boat, north.

ROSMER. Why north?

REBECCA. It's where I came from.

ROSMER. You've no one up there.

REBECCA. And who have I here?

ROSMER. What will you do?

REBECCA. I don't know. Have done with it, that's all I know.

ROSMER. Have done?

REBECCA. Rosmersholm has broken me.

ROSMER. Pardon?

REBECCA. Broken me in pieces. When I came I had freewill, spirit. Now strangers' customs have crushed me. I don't think I've the willpower to do anything else again, ever.

ROSMER. Customs, crushed you. What d'you mean?

REBECCA. Johannes, change the subject. What happened between you and Doctor Kroll?

ROSMER. We ended our quarrel.

REBECCA. I knew it.

ROSMER. He gathered all our old friends. They persuaded me. Ennobling people is no work for me. And in any case, it's impossible. I'll let it go.

REBECCA. Perhaps that's best.

ROSMER. Is *that* what you say? What you think?

REBECCA. These last few days.

ROSMER. Rebecca, you're lying.

REBECCA. Lying?

ROSMER. You've never had faith in me. Never thought I was the man to lead the cause to triumph.

REBECCA. The two of us together –

ROSMER. Nonsense. You thought *you* could do something magnificent. And you thought you'd use me, you'd thought I'd be useful. That's all it was.

REBECCA. Johannes, listen –

ROSMER (*wearily, sitting on the sofa*). Don't bother. I understand completely. I was . . . like a glove in your hands.

REBECCA. Listen, Johannes. We have to settle this. Forever.

She sits in a chair beside him.

I was going to write you a letter, when I was north again. But I'll tell you, now.

ROSMER. Not more confessions.

REBECCA. The most important.

ROSMER. What d'you mean?

REBECCA. The one you've never suspected. The one that explains all the others.

ROSMER. I don't know what you mean.

REBECCA. It's perfectly true that I set out to be taken on here at Rosmersholm. I thought I was sure to do well for myself, in one way or another.

ROSMER. You certainly succeeded.

REBECCA. I thought I could do anything I wanted, then. I had freewill, courage, nothing to stop me, no ties with another living soul. But then it began, and it's snapped me, broken me forever.

ROSMER. Then what began? Explain yourself.

REBECCA. Desire swept over me. Wild, I couldn't control it. Johannes –

ROSMER. What desire?

REBECCA. For you.

ROSMER. What is this?

He tries to get up. She stops him.

REBECCA. Please listen.

ROSMER. You felt . . . *love* for me?

REBECCA. I called it love, then. I thought it was love. But it wasn't. Uncontrollable desire.

ROSMER (*awkwardly*). Rebecca, *you* . . . ? You're talking about yourself?

REBECCA. Yes, Johannes. Imagine.

ROSMER. And it was because of this . . . driven by this . . . that you 'went to work', as you put it?

REBECCA. It was a storm. A North Sea storm. It sweeps you anywhere it chooses. No resisting it.

ROSMER. And poor Beata: it swept her into the millrace.

REBECCA. Then, it was her life or mine.

ROSMER. You were the strongest then. Of the three of us at Rosmersholm.

REBECCA. I knew you had to be free before I could reach you – literally; in spirit.

ROSMER. Rebecca, you baffle me. You yourself, everything you do, a mystery. I'm free now, literally, in spirit, you've got what you wanted, and still –

REBECCA. I've never been further from getting what I wanted.

ROSMER. I mean, yesterday when I asked you, begged you, to marry me, you said it was impossible. You were like someone screaming in terror.

REBECCA. In despair, Johannes.

ROSMER. Why?

REBECCA. Because Rosmersholm has broken me. Snatched my will. Unnerved me. I daren't do anything, not now. My dear, I'm powerless.

ROSMER. How did it happen?

REBECCA. Our life together.

ROSMER. What do you mean?

REBECCA. When I was alone with you here, when you recovered yourself . . .

ROSMER. Yes.

REBECCA. You were never yourself while Beata –

ROSMER. I understand.

REBECCA. When we shared everything here, peace, solitude, when you shared your thoughts, tenderly, intimately, I began to change. Slowly, imperceptibly, then irresistibly, to the bottom of my soul.

ROSMER. Rebecca, what are you – ?

REBECCA. The other thing, the desire, the intoxication, vanished. The whirling stopped, the passion. Stillness. The mountains, the midnight sun . . .

ROSMER. Tell me everything about it.

REBECCA. That's all. It was love, true love. Self-denying, contented with everything we had together.

ROSMER. I'd no idea. If only –

REBECCA. It's best as it is. Yesterday, when you asked me to marry you, I shouted for joy.

ROSMER. I knew it!

REBECCA. At first. I'd forgotten. My old self, my willpower, struggling to be free. But now it's faded, no strength left, nothing.

ROSMER. But I don't un –

REBECCA. The Rosmer view of life – your view of life – engulfed it.

ROSMER. Engulfed it?

REBECCA. Swallowed it, enslaved it. Customs I'd never known before. You – living with you – has ennobled me.

ROSMER. Oh, Rebecca!

REBECCA. It's what happens. The Rosmer view of life ennobles. And . . .

She shakes her head.

And it –

ROSMER. What?

REBECCA. And it kills all happiness.

ROSMER. You think so?

REBECCA. For me it does.

ROSMER. Are you sure? If I asked you again . . . if I begged you, now, went down on my knees and begged you –

REBECCA. Johannes, no. Don't mention it again. It's impossible. My dear, I . . . passion . . . in the past I . . . I've given way before.

ROSMER. Something else you didn't tell me.

REBECCA. Something else. Important. Yes.

ROSMER. Imagine, Rebecca. I did wonder. It did cross my mind.

REBECCA. And even so you – ?

ROSMER. Crossed my mind, I said. Not serious.

REBECCA. I'll tell you. Shall I tell you?

ROSMER. No. I don't want to hear. It's not important.

REBECCA. It is to me.

ROSMER. Oh Rebecca –

REBECCA. This is the worst thing. My feelings have changed,
    I can reach out and touch all happiness – and my own
    past life prevents me.

ROSMER. Rebecca, your past is dead. Irrelevant, you've
    changed. No hold on you.

REBECCA. My dear, empty phrases. What about innocence,
    free conscience? Where's that to come from?

ROSMER (*wanly*). Free conscience.

REBECCA. The source of all peace, all happiness. You said.
    The truth you wanted to plant in the new generation. To
    make them happy, ennoble them.

ROSMER. That's not important. A dream, a childish notion,
    I've forgotten it. Rebecca, we can't be ennobled from
    outside ourselves.

REBECCA. Not even by love, love in gentleness?

ROSMER. If that could be . . . the one thing above all
    others, the one great thing . . . (*Uneasily.*) But how can
    I know? How can I be sure?

REBECCA. Johannes, don't you trust me?

ROSMER. How *can* I trust you? All this time you've been
    hiding things, pretending. Now this. What is it you want?
    Tell me. I'll do anything I can for you.

REBECCA. Johannes . . . trust . . . you can't trust . . .

ROSMER. How can I help it? It gnaws at me. How can
    I ever be sure? Pure, perfect love – how can I know?

REBECCA. My dear: your heart, your heart of hearts. Don't
    you see I've changed, thanks to you, to no one else, to you?

ROSMER. I've lost faith, in my power to change others, in myself, in you.

REBECCA (*with a glance of foreboding at him*). Then how can you live?

ROSMER. I don't know. I've no idea. I don't see how I can. There's nothing in the world worth living for.

REBECCA. Life, Johannes, it soon renews itself. While we can, let's seize it.

ROSMER. Then give me back my faith. Rebecca, faith in you, in your love. Give me proof, please proof . . .

REBECCA. How can I?

ROSMER. You have to. I can't stand this. Desolation, emptiness . . . I –

Loud knocking, off. REBECCA *jumps up.*

REBECCA. What is it?

Enter ULRIK BRENDEL. *He is wearing a white shirt, black coat and good boots, with his trousers tucked into them. But otherwise he is dressed as in Act One. He is wildly excited.*

ROSMER. Mr Brendel!

BRENDEL. Johannes, dear boy, goodbye forever.

ROSMER. Where are you going, at this time of night?

BRENDEL. Down the dark road.

ROSMER. Pardon?

BRENDEL. Home, darling boy, I'm homesick. I yearn for Oblivion, the Dark.

ROSMER. What's happened to you?

BRENDEL. You observe the transformation? And well you might. When last I bestrode these halls, I stood before you a man of substance, with ducats in my purse.

ROSMER. I don't –

BRENDEL. But now, I come before you now, a monarch dethroned, on the ash-heap I called my palace.

ROSMER. If there's anything –

BRENDEL. You have the innocence of a child, dear boy. A loan perhaps?

ROSMER. As much as you want.

BRENDEL. An ideal or two?

ROSMER. Pardon?

BRENDEL. Cast-off ideals? From the kindness of your heart. I'm ruined, dear boy, cleaned out, in penury.

REBECCA. Didn't you give your lecture?

BRENDEL. Charming lady, no. Picture the scene. There I was, preparing to pour from the horn of plenty, and I find to my distress, I'm bankrupt.

REBECCA. But the books you were going to write –

BRENDEL. For five and twenty years I've sat like a miser on his treasure-chest. And yesterday, when I open it and want to disburse from it, it's empty. Ground to dust by the teeth of time. All that finery, reduced to nix, nought, nothing!

ROSMER. You're certain?

BRENDEL. No room for doubt, young fellow. The President himself assured me.

ROSMER. What president?

BRENDEL. His Excellency. The Dear Beloved.

ROSMER. But what's his name?

BRENDEL. Why, Peder Mortensgård.

ROSMER. What?

BRENDEL (*mysteriously*). Sh! Sh! Peder Mortensgård, Lord and Master of the Future. Never have I been admitted to a more imposing presence. Peder Mortensgård has the secret of omnipotence. He can do anything he chooses.

ROSMER. That's nonsense.

BRENDEL. No, no, dear boy. Mr Mortensgård never aims further than he can reach. He's learned how to live without ideals. *That's* the secret: action and victory, the wisdom of the world. Hoopla!

ROSMER. Now I understand why you're leaving us poorer than when you came.

BRENDEL. *Eh bien. Quod erat demonstrandum.* Learn the lesson. Expunge from your mind all your ancient tutor imprinted there. Build not your house on shifting sand. Look to the future, test every step before you make it, before you build on this delightful being who sweetens your entire existence.

REBECCA. You mean me.

BRENDEL. Enchantress, indeed I do.

REBECCA. Why am I not to be built on?

BRENDEL (*taking a step nearer*). It's come to my attention that my former pupil has a cause, a cause to carry through to triumph.

REBECCA. Yes?

BRENDEL. Triumph is assured. But, mark me well, on one condition.

REBECCA. What condition?

BRENDEL (*taking her gently by the wrist*). That the young woman who adores him goes out to the kitchen, with gladness in her heart, and chops off her soft, white little finger: this one, here at the joint. Then, that the aforesaid adoring young woman – equally with gladness in her heart – slices off her shell-like left ear.

He lets her go and turns to ROSMER.

All-conquering, adieu!

ROSMER. You're going now? It's dark.

BRENDEL. When better? Peace upon you both.

Exit. Pause. REBECCA *is breathing hard.*

REBECCA. It's so stuffy in here!

She opens the window, and stands there. ROSMER *sits in the chair by the stove.*

ROSMER. There's no other way, Rebecca. You have to leave.

REBECCA. No other way.

ROSMER. Let's make the most of what time we have left. Sit beside me.

REBECCA *sits on the sofa.*

REBECCA. What is it, Johannes?

ROSMER. I want to tell you, first, that you needn't worry about your future.

REBECCA (*with a smile*). *My* future . . .

ROSMER. I arranged everything long ago. Whatever happens, you're provided for.

REBECCA. How kind you are.

ROSMER. You should have realised.

REBECCA. It's been years since I –

ROSMER. You thought nothing between us would ever change.

REBECCA. Yes.

ROSMER. So did I. But if I die –

REBECCA. Johannes, you'll live longer than I will.

ROSMER. I think that's up to me. What's it worth, my life?

REBECCA. You're not thinking – ?

ROSMER. Are you surprised? After this miserable, pitiful defeat? I was to carry a great cause to triumph – and I ran from the battle before it even started.

REBECCA. Johannes, take it up again. Just try, you'll triumph. Your mission – you'll ennoble hundreds, thousands . . . Only try!

ROSMER. My mission: I think I've lost faith in that.

REBECCA. It's stood the test already. You've ennobled one human being already: me. For the rest of my days.

ROSMER. If I dared believe you . . .

REBECCA (*pressing her hands together*). Johannes, is there no way to make you believe it?

ROSMER (*starts as if afraid*). Don't ask that, Rebecca. We mustn't talk of it.

REBECCA. We must. Do *you* know a way to kill the doubt in you? *I* don't.

ROSMER. Then leave it that way. Best for you, for both of us.

REBECCA. Don't stop me. If there's anything, if you know of anything, that would let you forgive me, tell me. You owe it to me.

ROSMER (*reluctantly*). All right. You say you're full of love, I've ennobled your mind. D'you mean that? Is it exact? Can it be proved? Tell me!

REBECCA. I'm ready.

ROSMER. When?

REBECCA. When you decide. The sooner the –

ROSMER. This evening, then. Would you, for my sake, this evening – (*Breaking off.*) It's no good.

REBECCA. I'll prove it, Johannes. Tell me.

ROSMER. Have you the courage, the willpower – with gladness in your heart, as Ulrik Brendel put it – for my sake, with gladness in your heart, to go where Beata went?

REBECCA (*getting up slowly, almost voiceless*). Johannes . . .

ROSMER. When you've left Rosmersholm, that question will haunt me. Every moment of the day. I see you standing there . . . on the bridge . . . halfway across . . . leaning over the handrail . . . dizzy, it beckons you, the millrace beckoning . . . No. You pull back. You haven't the courage, *her* courage.

REBECCA. But if I had? If I did it, with gladness in my heart? What then?

ROSMER. Then I'd believe you. I'd have faith in you again. In my mission. My power to ennoble human souls. In the soul's ability to be ennobled.

REBECCA *covers her head with her shawl, and says calmly*:

REBECCA. You'll have your faith again.

ROSMER. Rebecca, are you brave enough . . . ?

REBECCA. You'll know tomorrow, or afterwards, when they recover my body.

ROSMER (*putting his hand to his forehead*). It's horrible . . . bewitching . . .

REBECCA. I don't want to stay down there. Longer than I have to. You must make sure they find me.

ROSMER (*jumping up*). This is lunacy. Leave Rosmersholm! Stay! I believe you, I trust you, whatever you say.

REBECCA. Words, Johannes. Evasions. After today, would you believe another word I said?

ROSMER. I won't see you defeated!

REBECCA. I won't be defeated.

ROSMER. You'll never go where Beata went.

REBECCA. Don't you think so?

ROSMER. You're not like her. Not ruled by a distorted view of life.

REBECCA. But ruled by the Rosmersholm view. I'm guilty. I have to pay.

ROSMER. You've decided.

REBECCA. Yes.

ROSMER (*firmly, his mind made up*). Freewill, Rebecca. Free choice. Like you, I stand decided. There's no judge to judge us, we must judge ourselves.

REBECCA (*not understanding*). Exactly. To save what's best in you, I have to go.

ROSMER. There's nothing left to save.

REBECCA. There is. But after today, all I'd be is a sea-witch, dragging you down. You have to go forward! I have to go overboard. What alternative? Go to and fro in the world, dragging my broken life, brooding on the happiness my past destroyed forever? Johannes, my part in this is over.

ROSMER. If you go, I go beside you.

REBECCA (*with an almost imperceptible smile, softly*). Come and watch me.

ROSMER. I said: go beside you.

REBECCA. As far as the bridge. You know you always avoid it.

ROSMER. You noticed?

REBECCA. That's what made my love hopeless.

ROSMER. Rebecca, I lay my hand on your head . . .

He does so.

I take you to be my true and lawful wife.

REBECCA *takes his hands and leans on his breast.*

REBECCA. Thank you.

She lets go.

Now I go, with gladness in my heart.

ROSMER. Husband and wife, together.

REBECCA. As far as the bridge.

ROSMER. And on to it. As far as you go, I go. Now, I dare.

REBECCA. Are you certain. This way is best?

ROSMER. It's best.

REBECCA. You're not mistaken? A fantasy? The White Horses of Rosmersholm?

ROSMER. Maybe. We can't escape them. All of us from Rosmersholm.

REBECCA. If that's so, stay!

ROSMER. Husband with wife, and wife with husband.

REBECCA. Tell me: are you with me, or am I with you?

ROSMER. We'll never know the answer.

REBECCA. I'd like to know.

ROSMER. Together, Rebecca: I with you and you with me.

REBECCA. I almost believe it.

ROSMER. The two of us are one.

REBECCA. One, yes. In gladness of heart.

Hand in hand, they go into the hall, and we see them turn left. They leave the hall doors open. Pause. Then MRS HELSETH *comes in right.*

MRS HELSETH. Miss West, the carriage is –

She looks round.

Not here? The pair of them out this time of night? Really!

She goes into the hall, looks round, comes back.

Not in the garden. Well, well.

She's at the window.

Ah! That white thing . . . They're on the bridge. God save them, they're in each other's arms. (*Shrieking.*) Ah! Down, both of them. The millrace. Help! Help!

She is overcome. She holds the chairback to support her trembling. She can scarcely speak.

No use. No help. The dead one took them.

End of the play.

Guide to Pronunciation of Names

Beata	bay-AH-ta
Helseth	HEL-set
Johannes	Yo-HA-nes
Lars	LARSH
Lauritz	LOW-rits ('as in English 'how')
Mortensgård	MOR-tens-gohr
Peder	PAY-der
Rosmersholm	ROS-mers-holm (short 'o' as in 'hot', and pronounce the 'l', ie not 'home')
Ulrik	OOL-reek